SLOTH COLORING BOOK

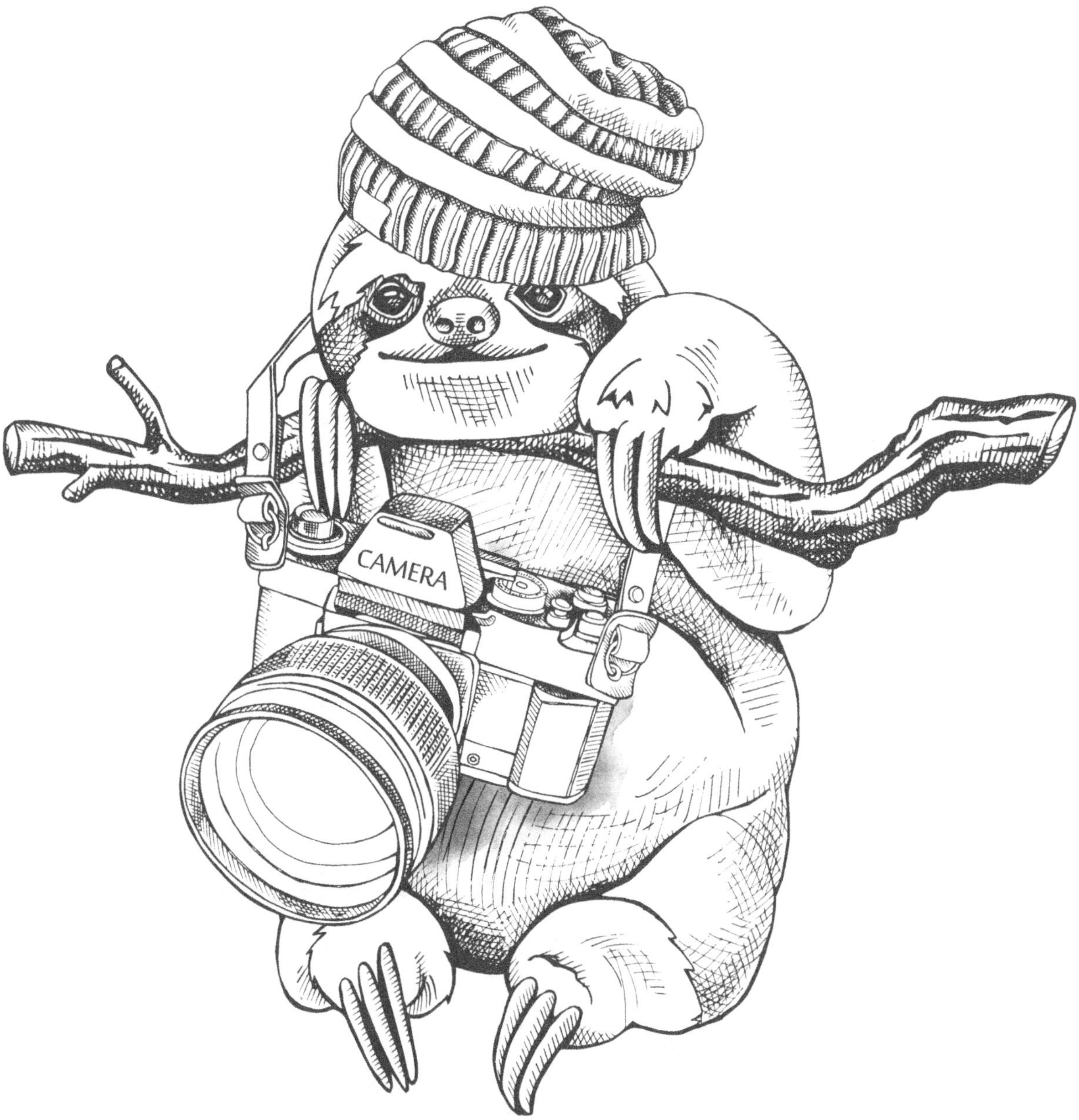

- RUSS FOCUS -

ISBN-13: 978-1727087840 ISBN-10: 1727087844

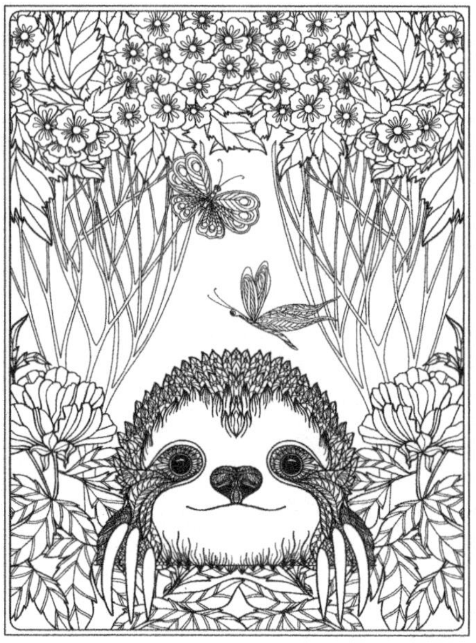
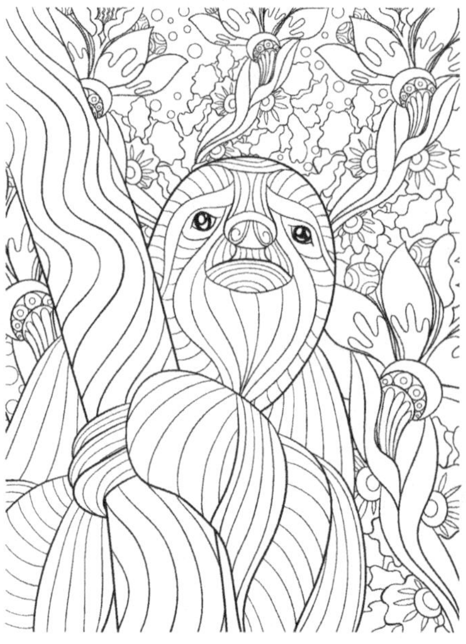
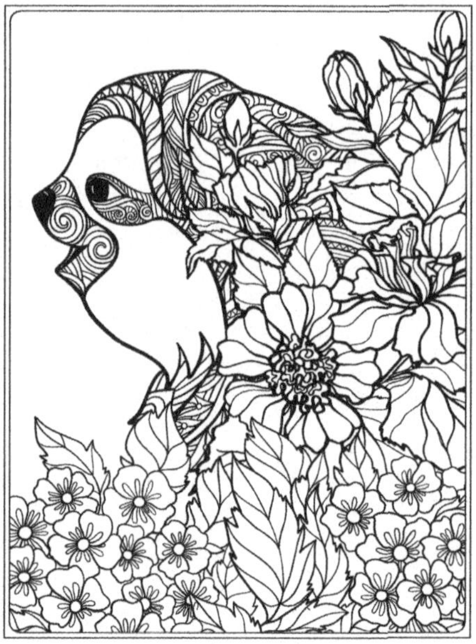
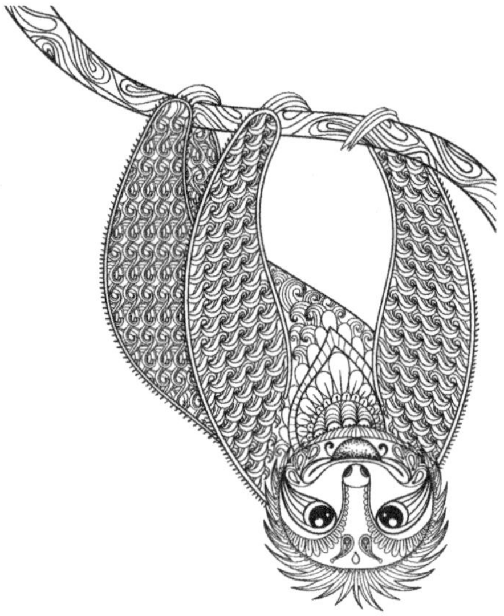

SAMPLE
SLOTH
COLORING
17 of 35
PAGES

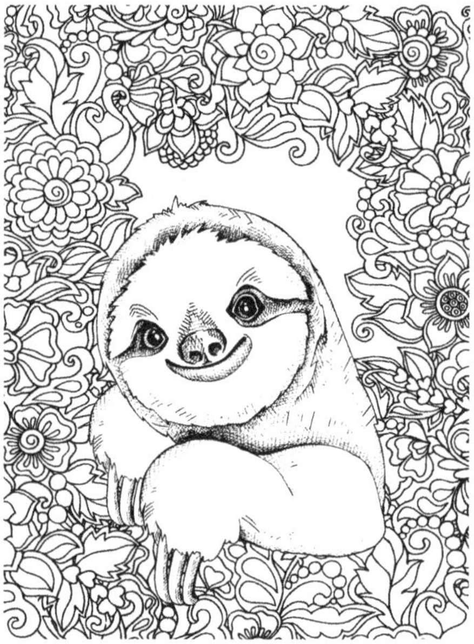
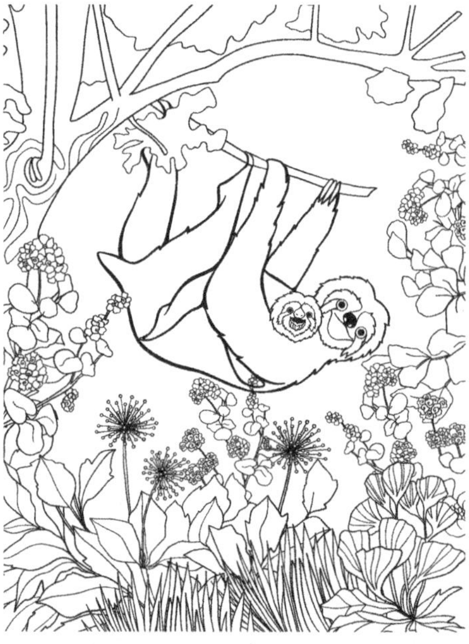
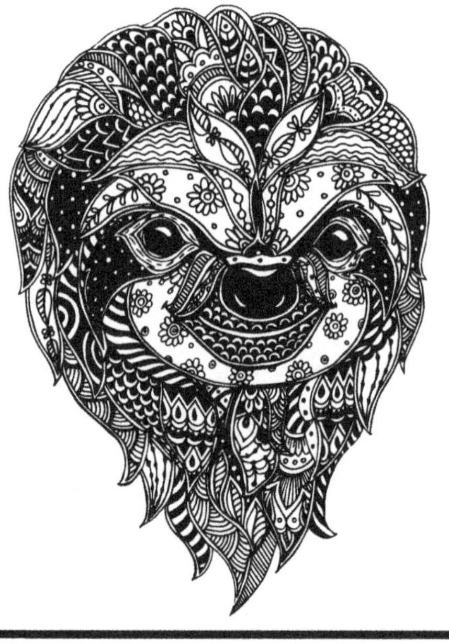
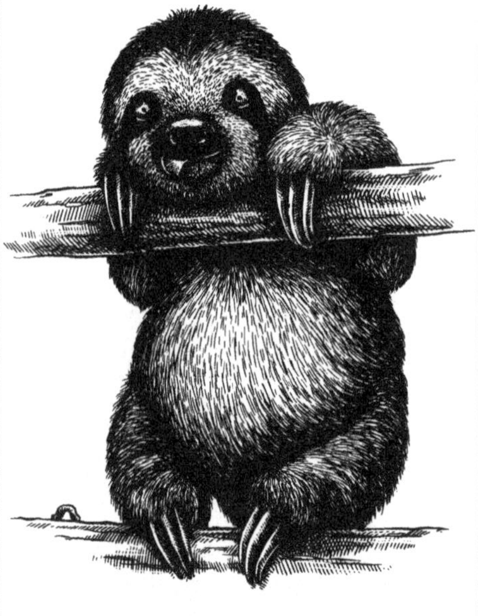

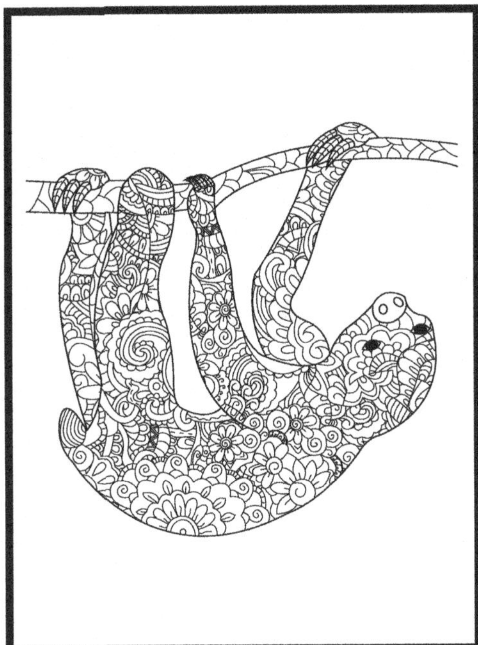
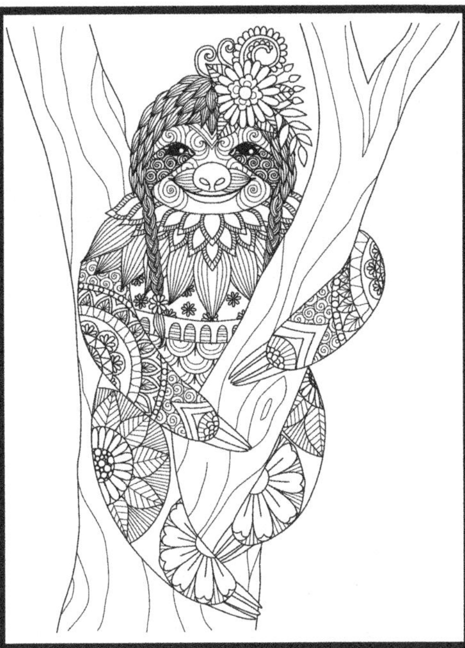
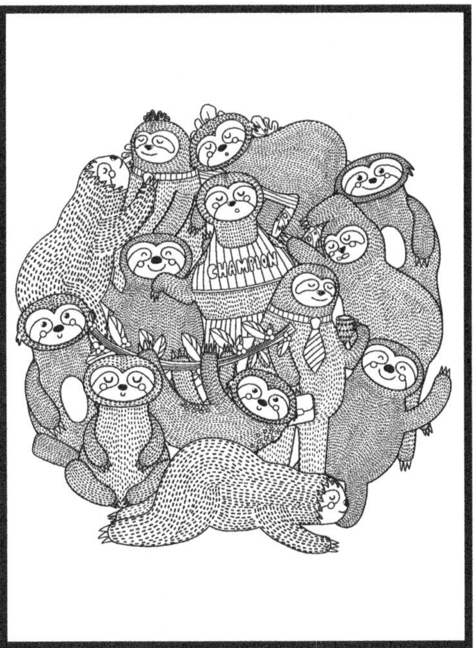
CHAMPION
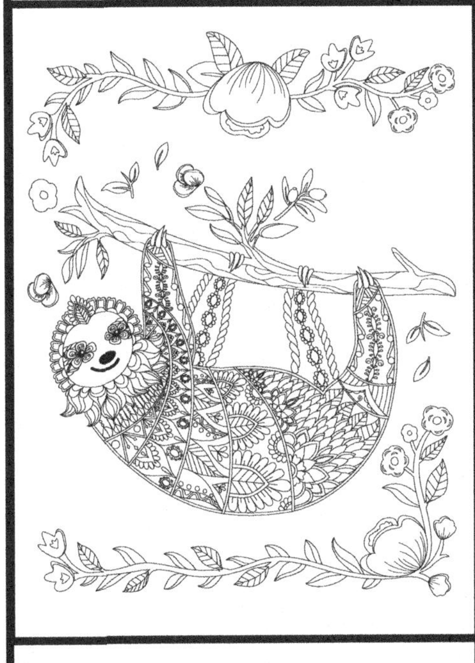
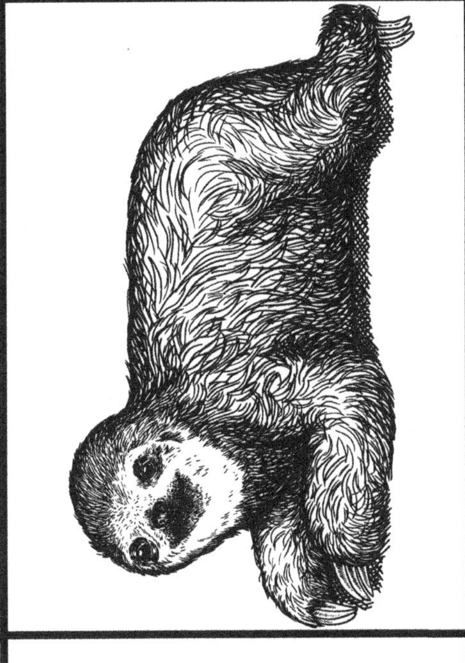
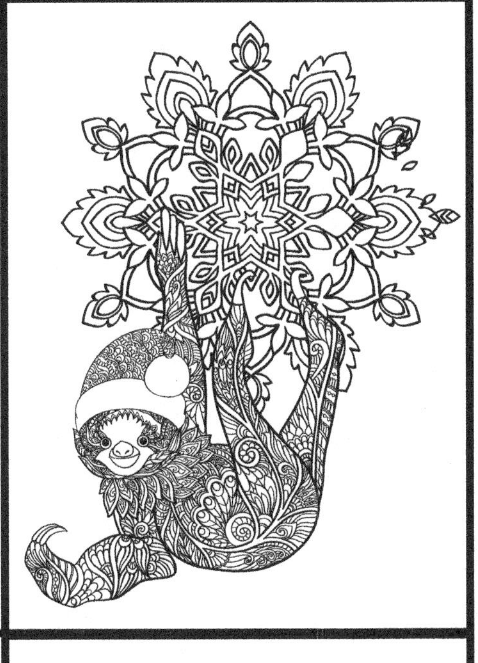
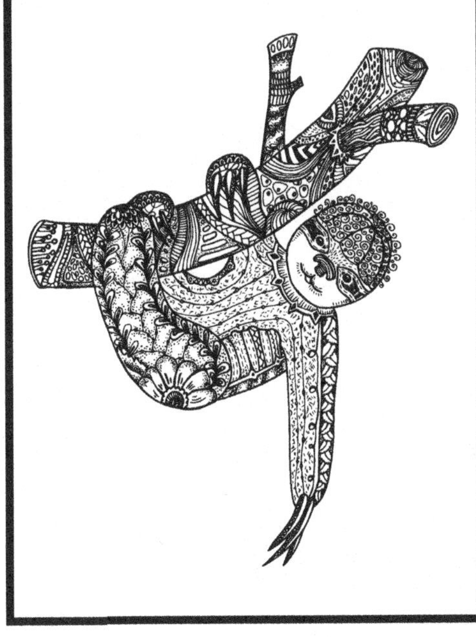
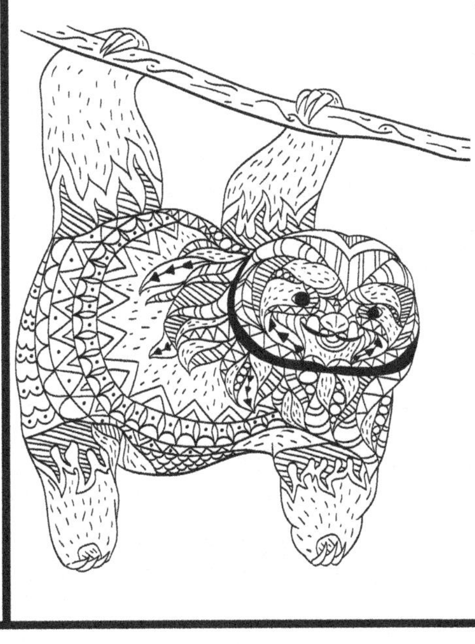
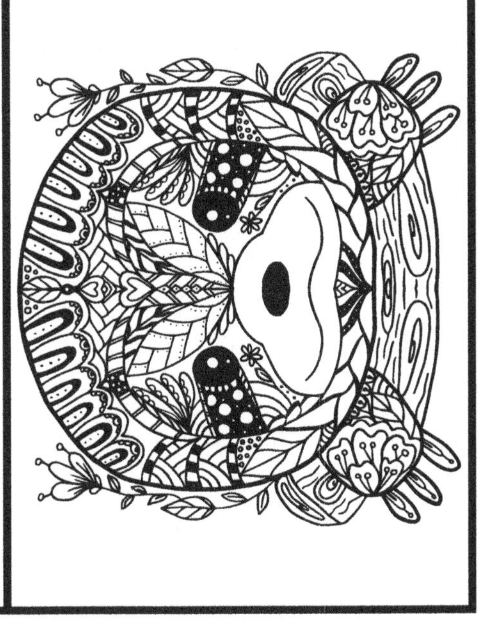

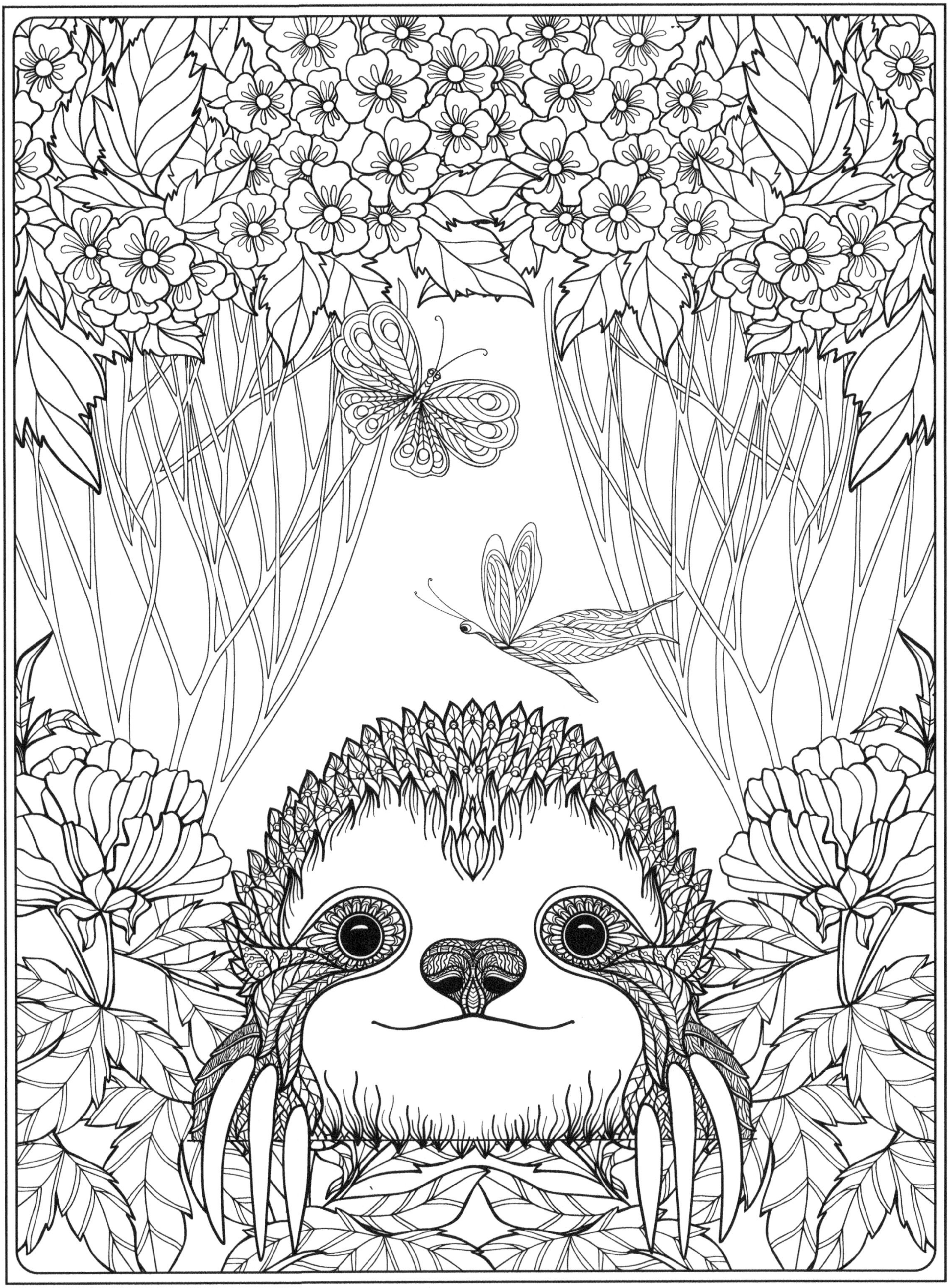

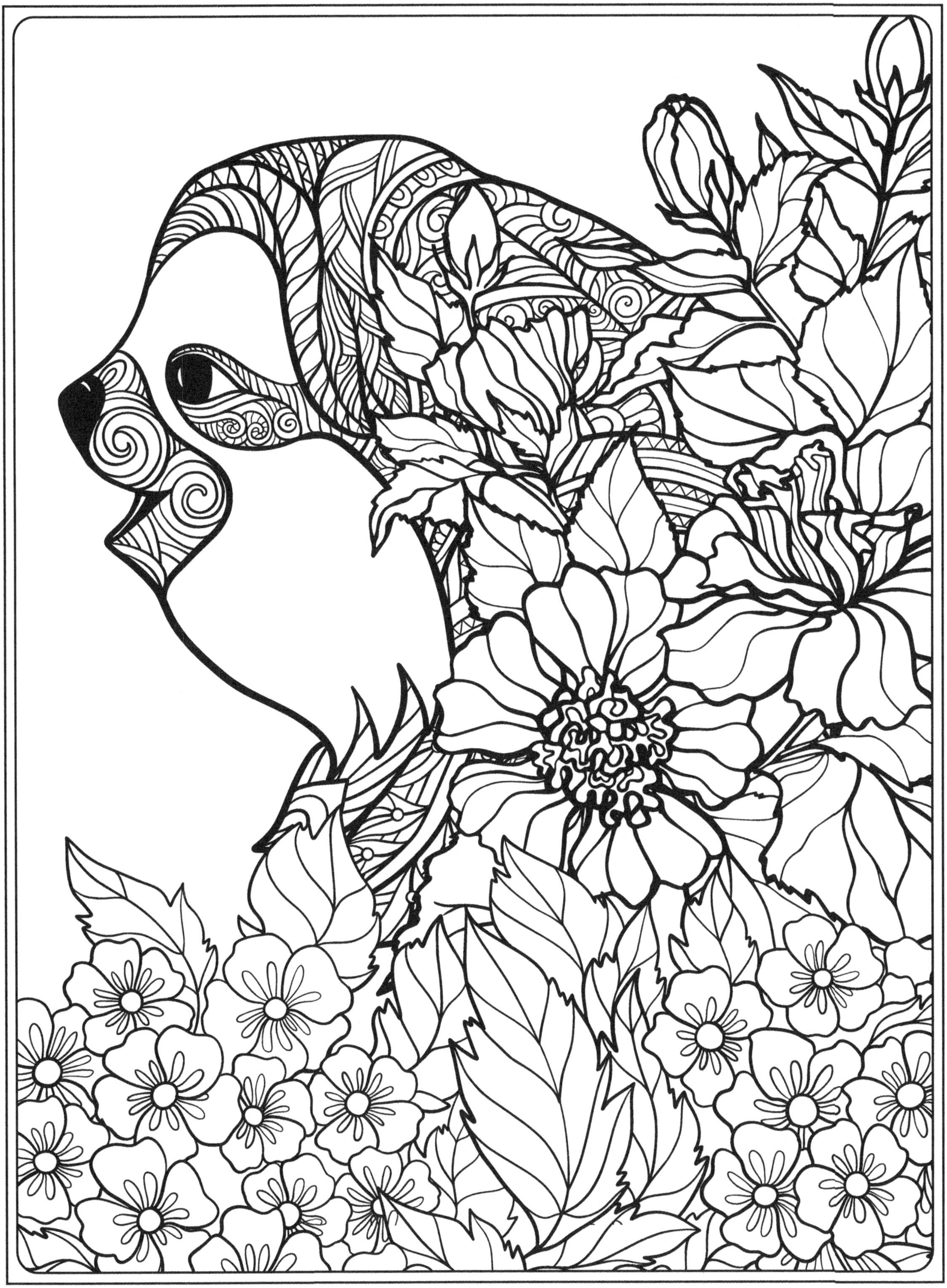

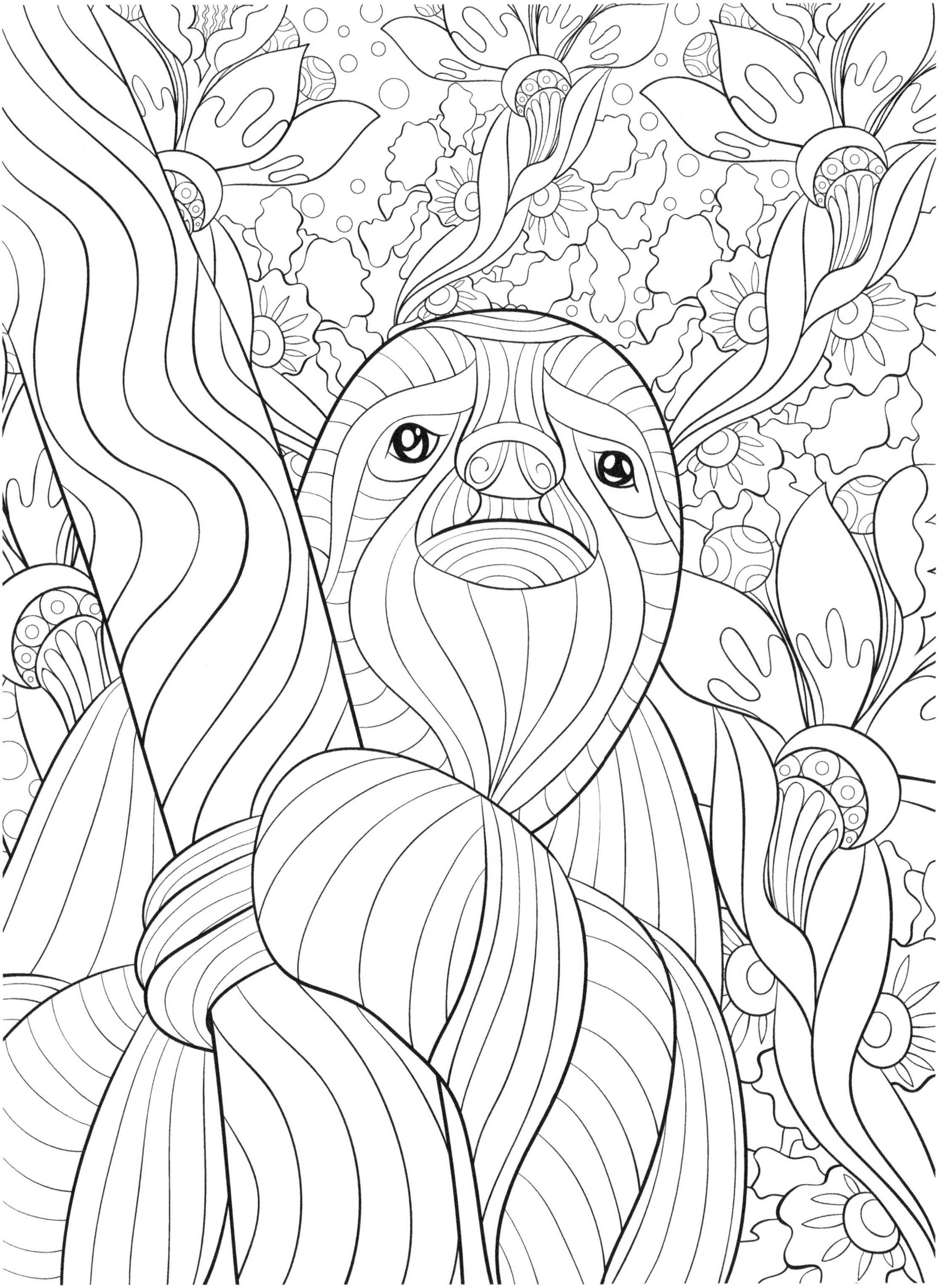

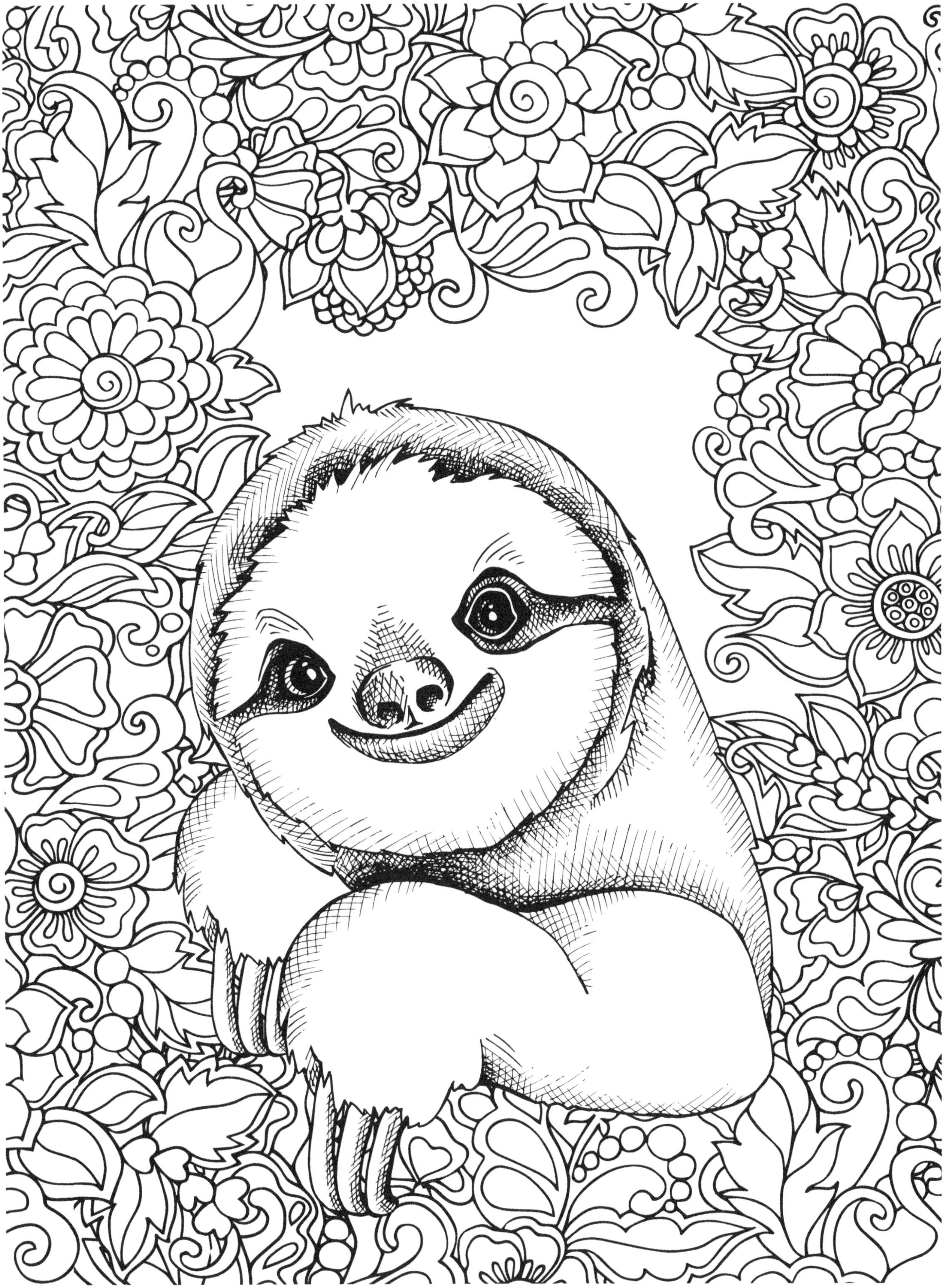

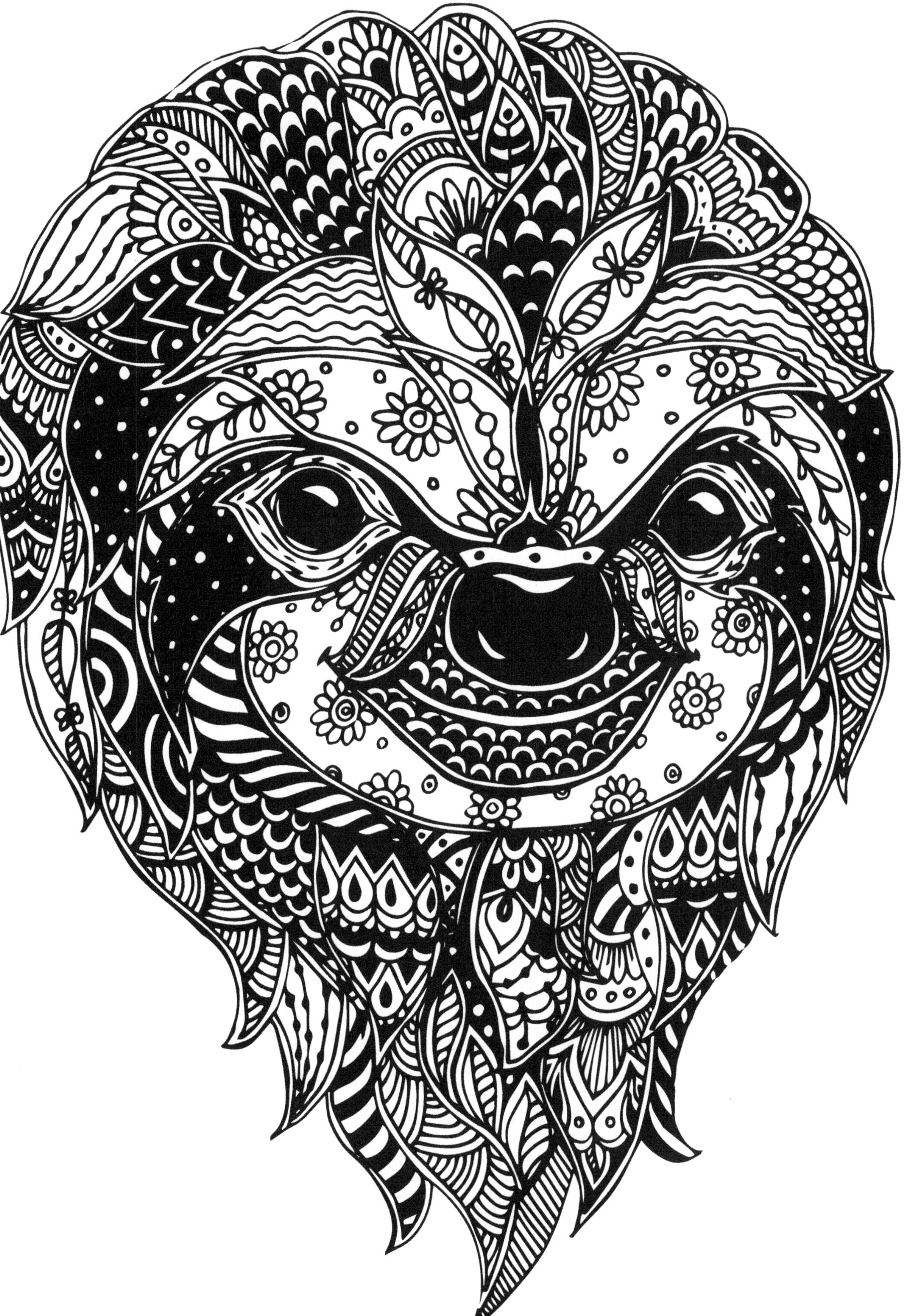

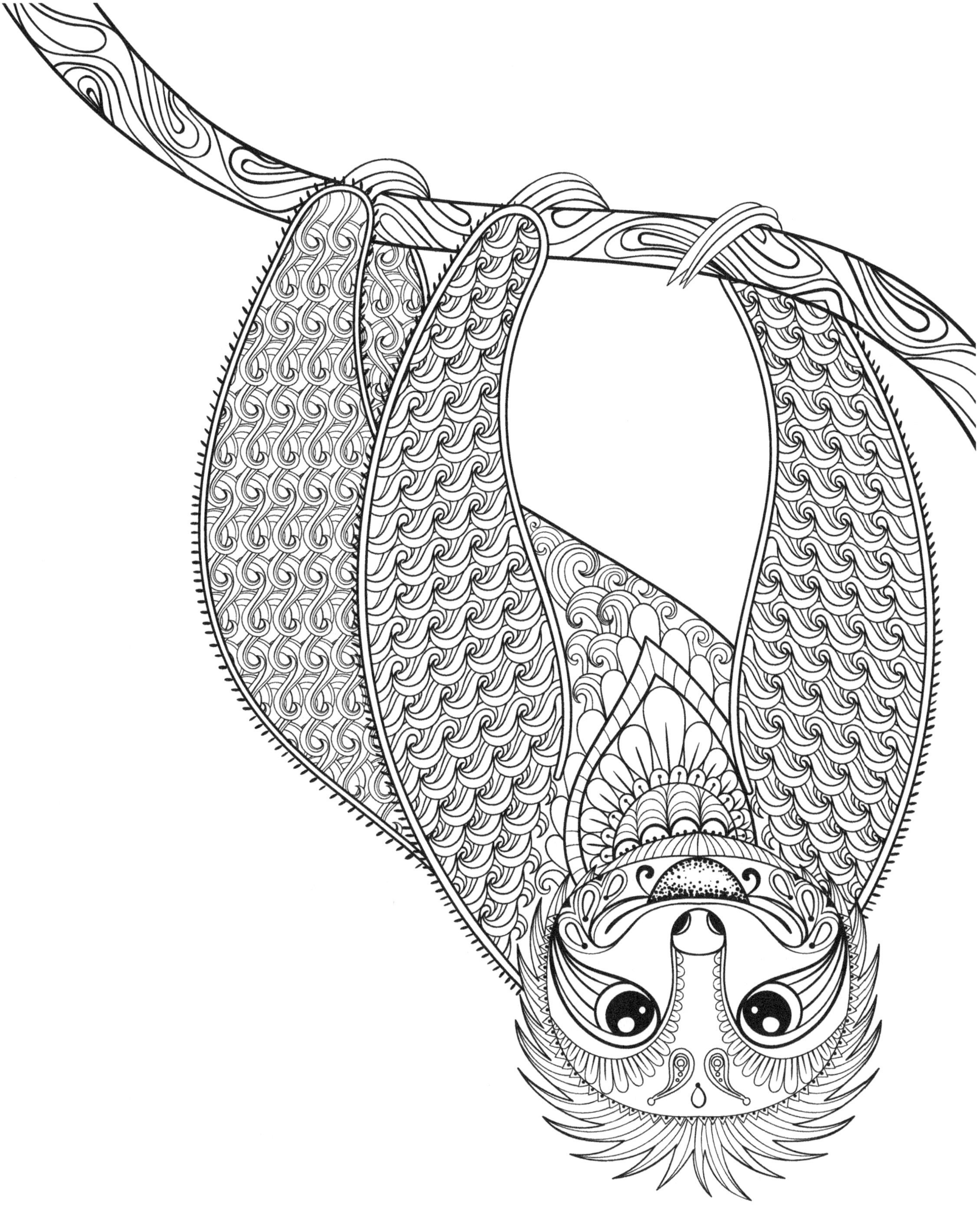

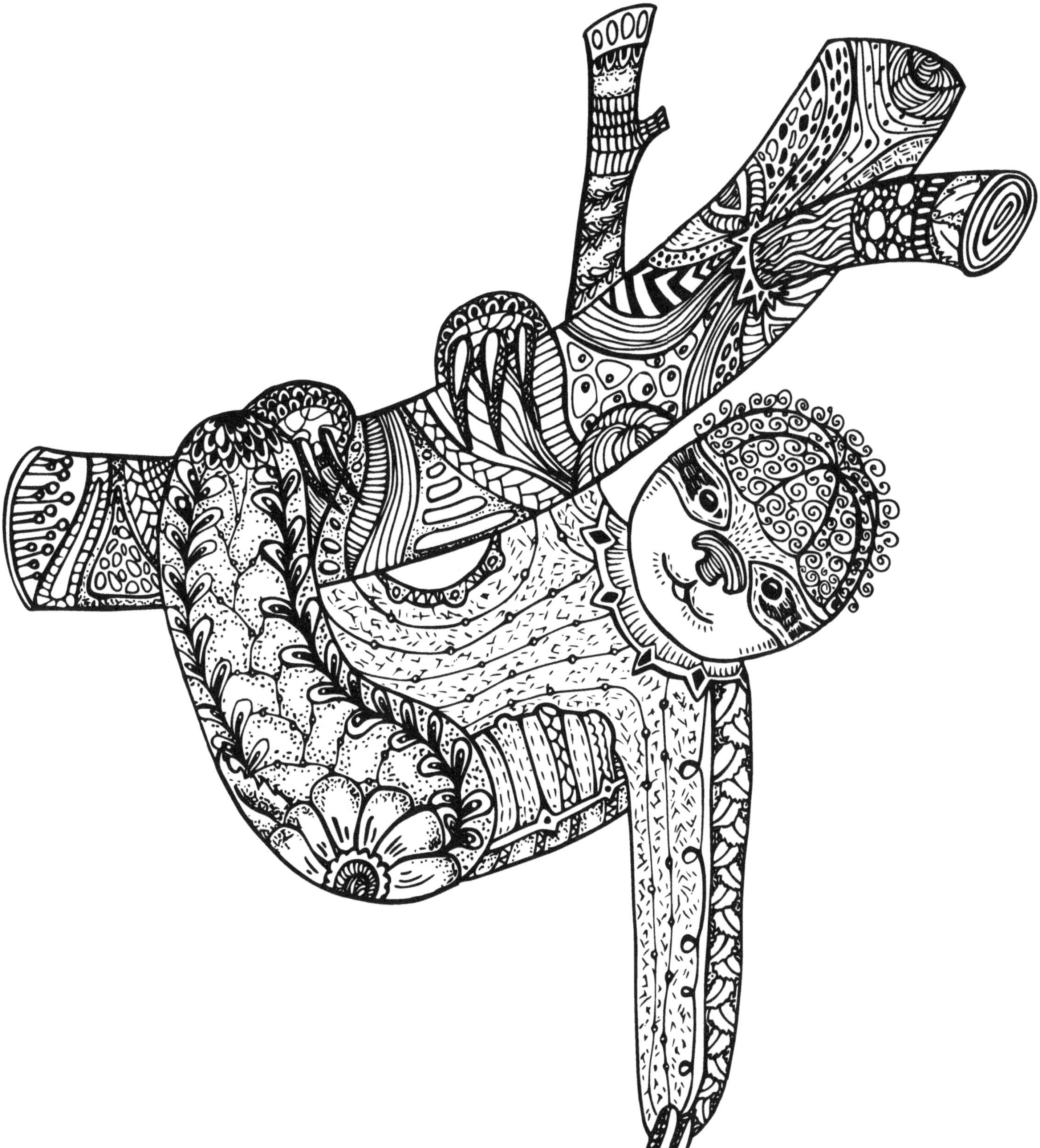

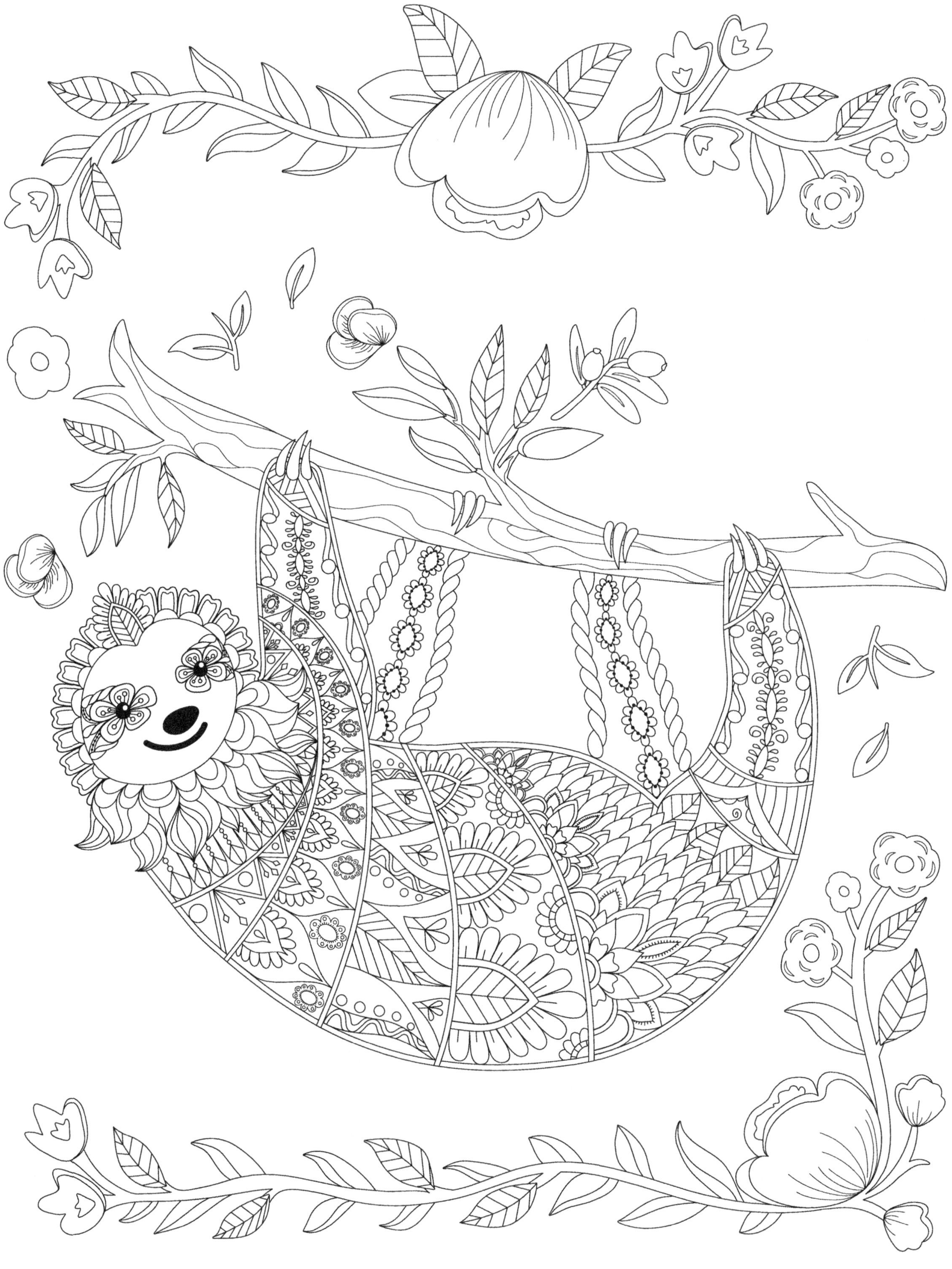

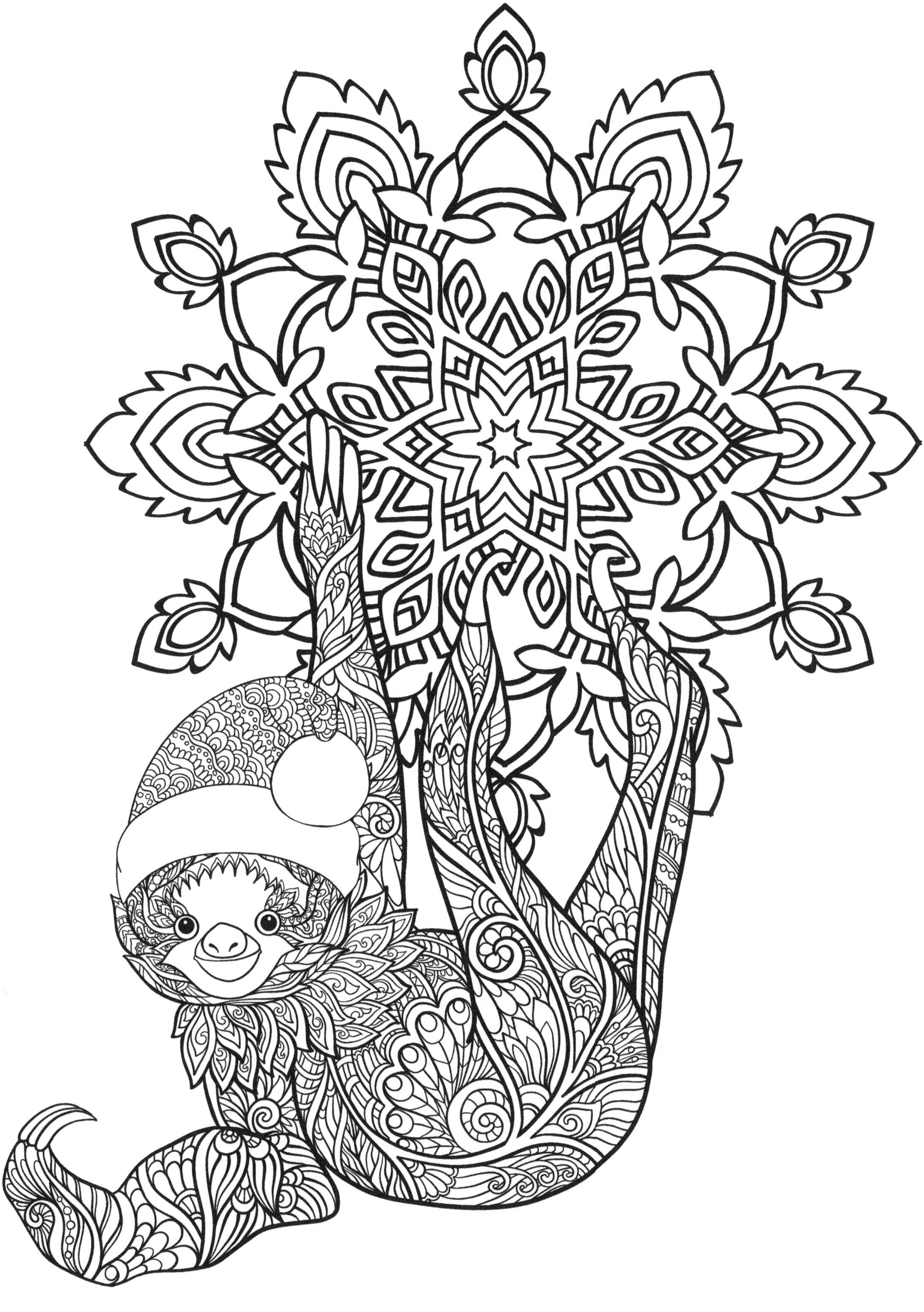

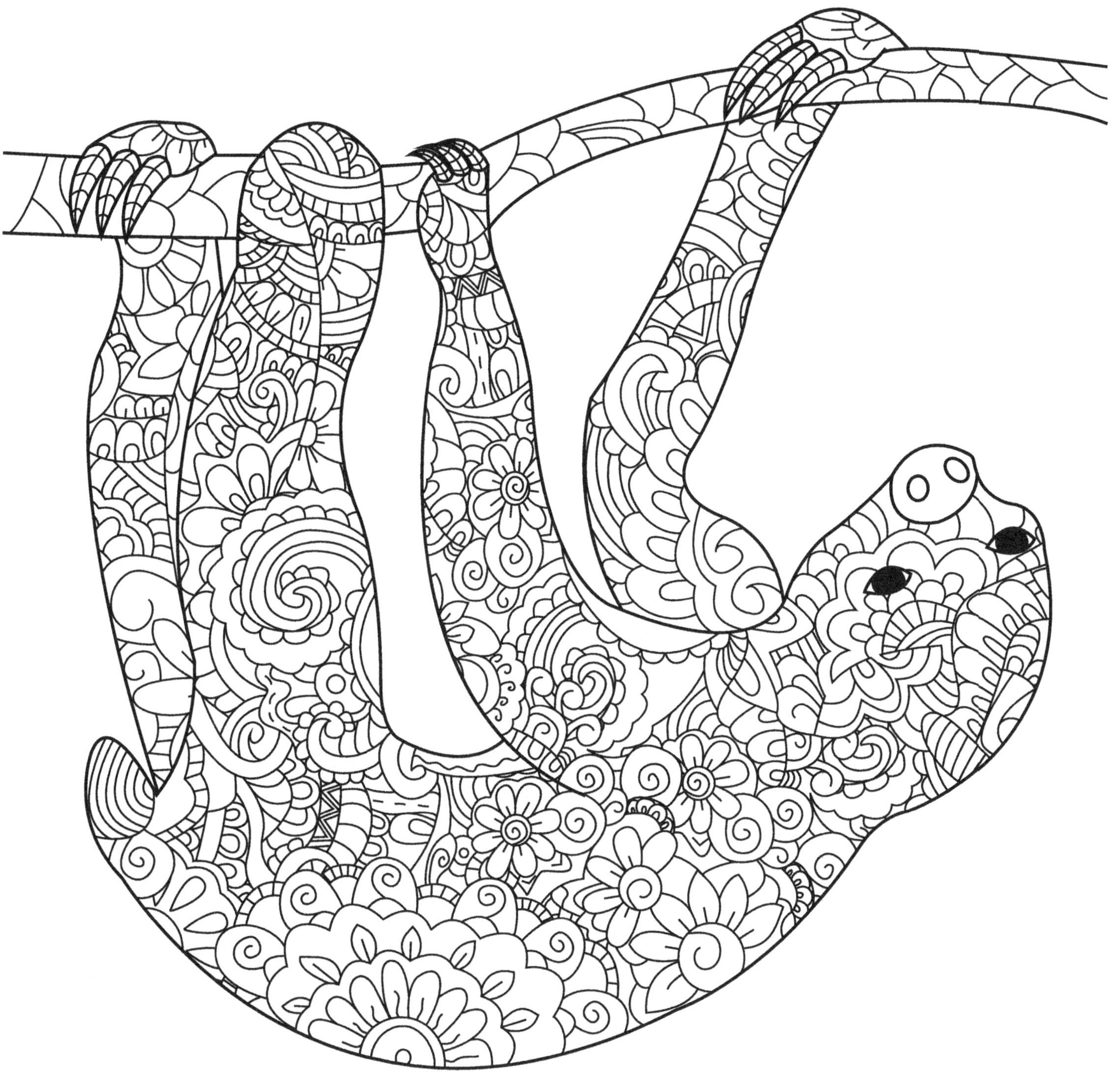

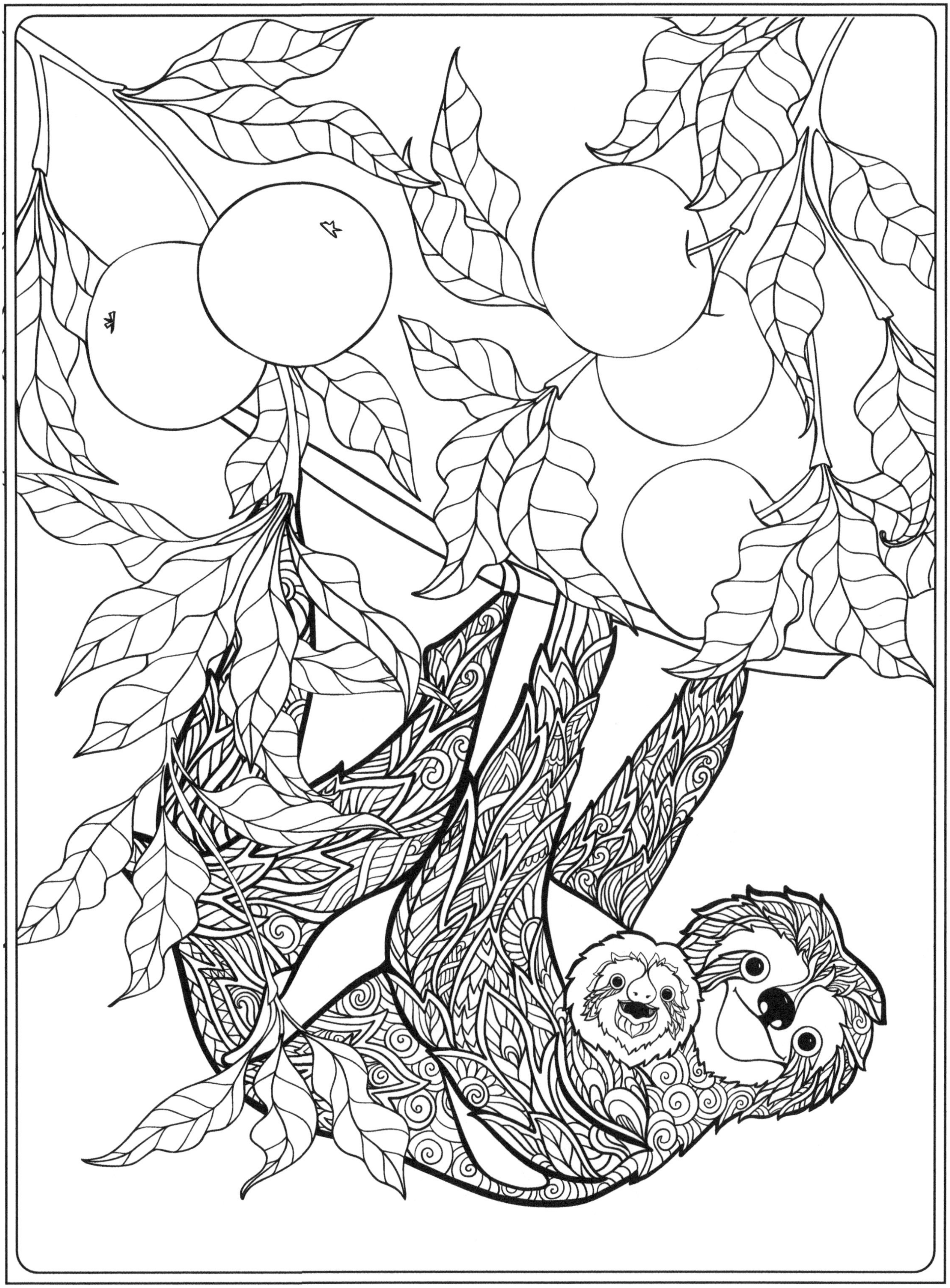

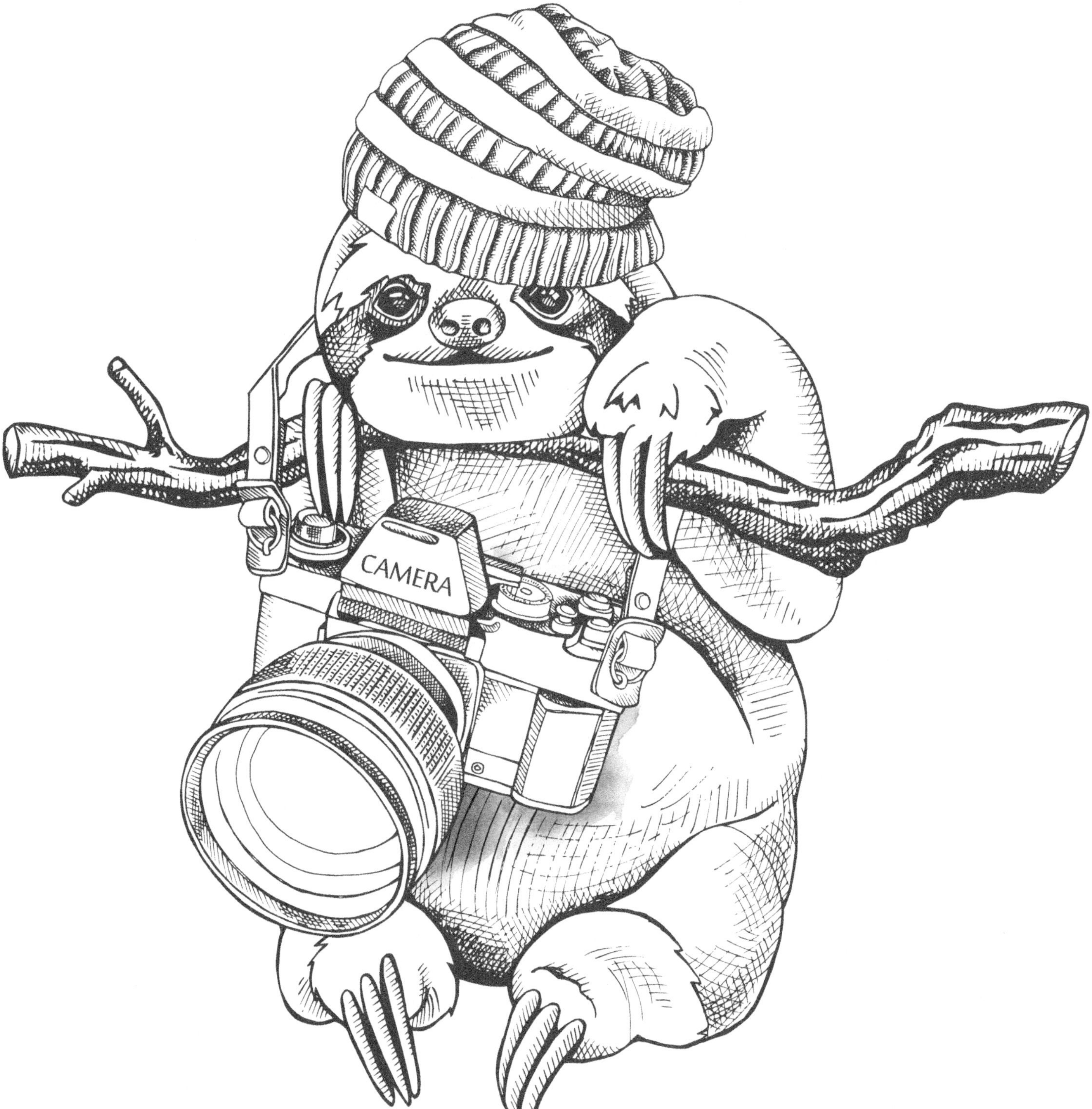
CAMERA

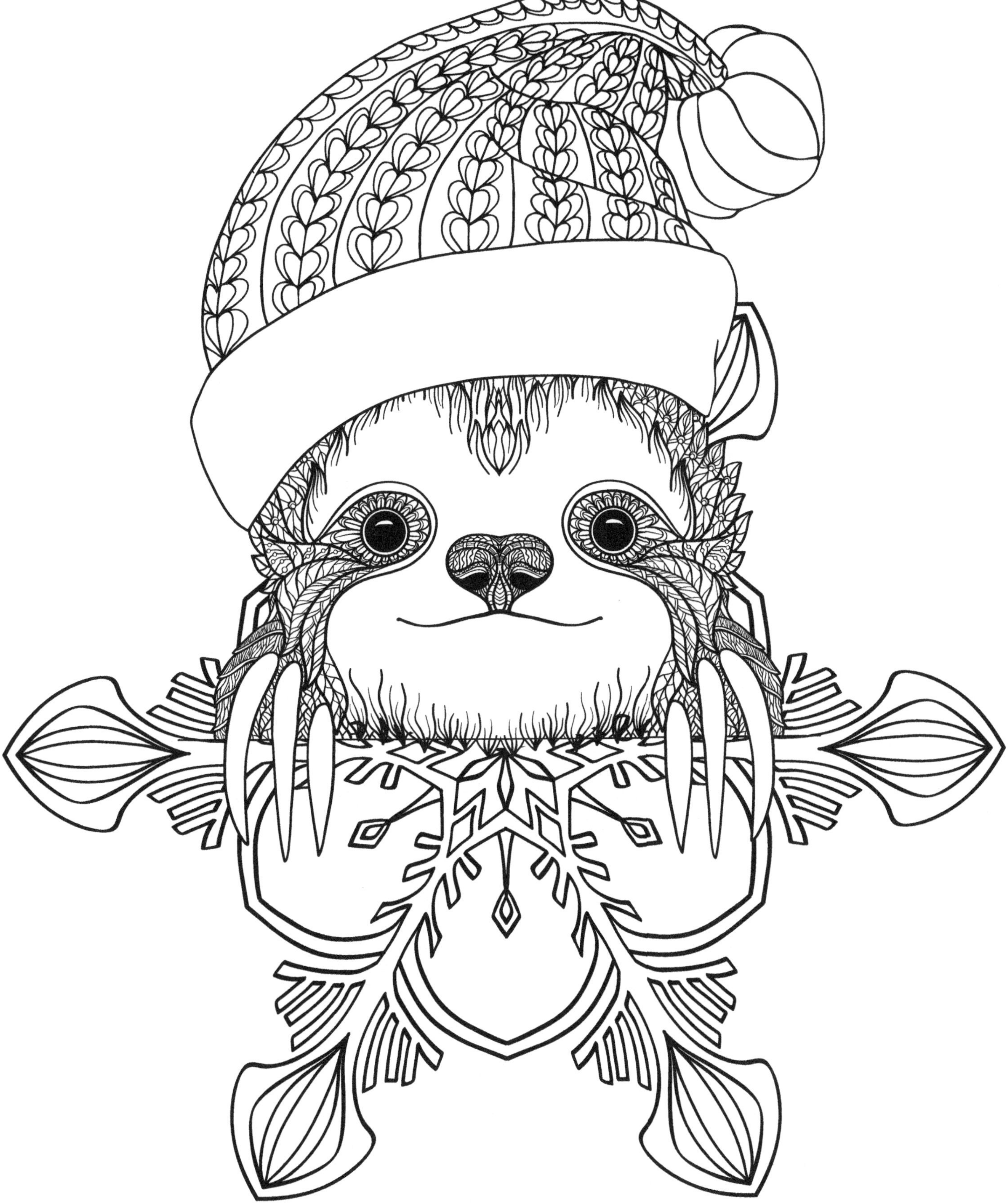

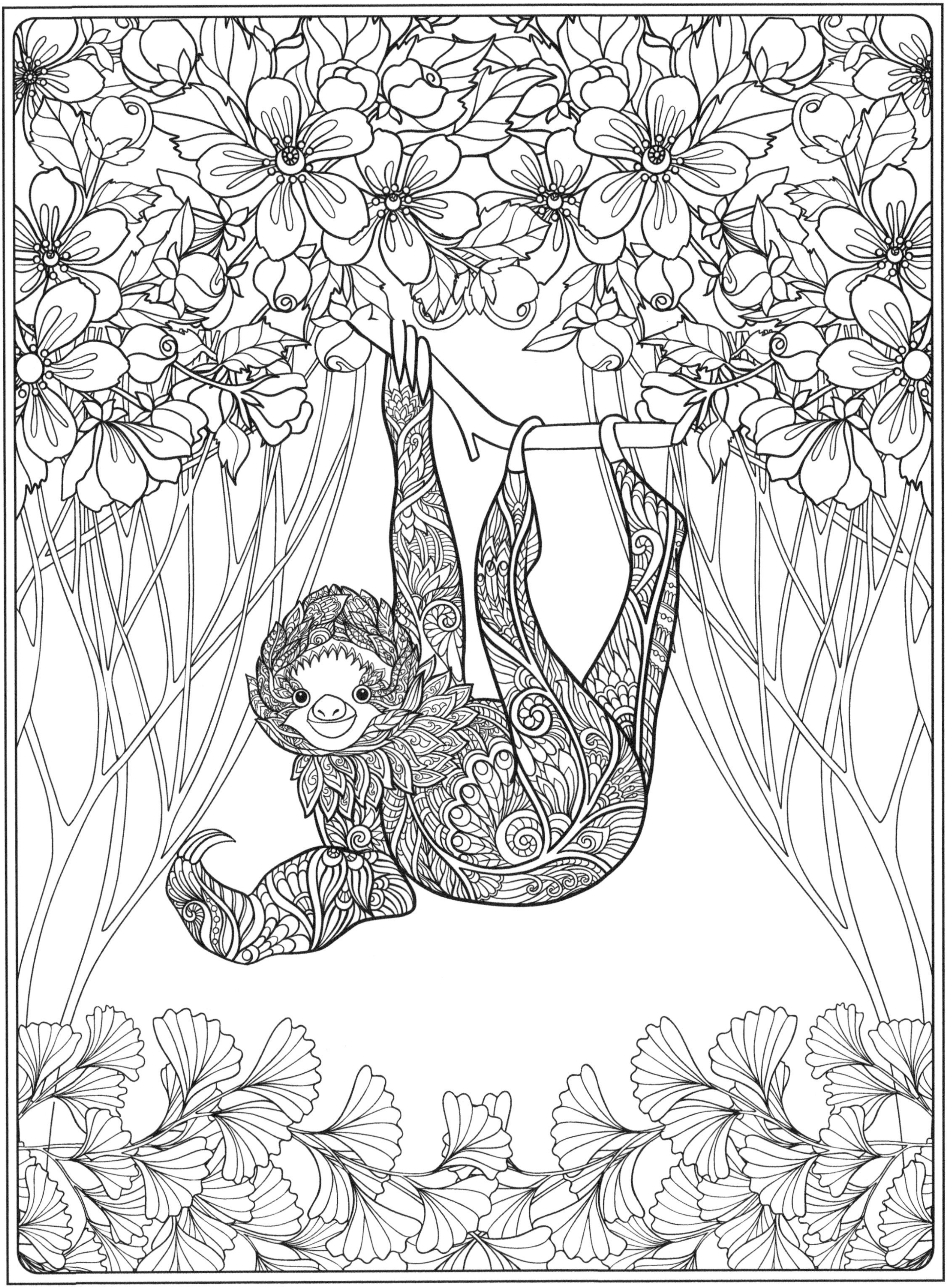

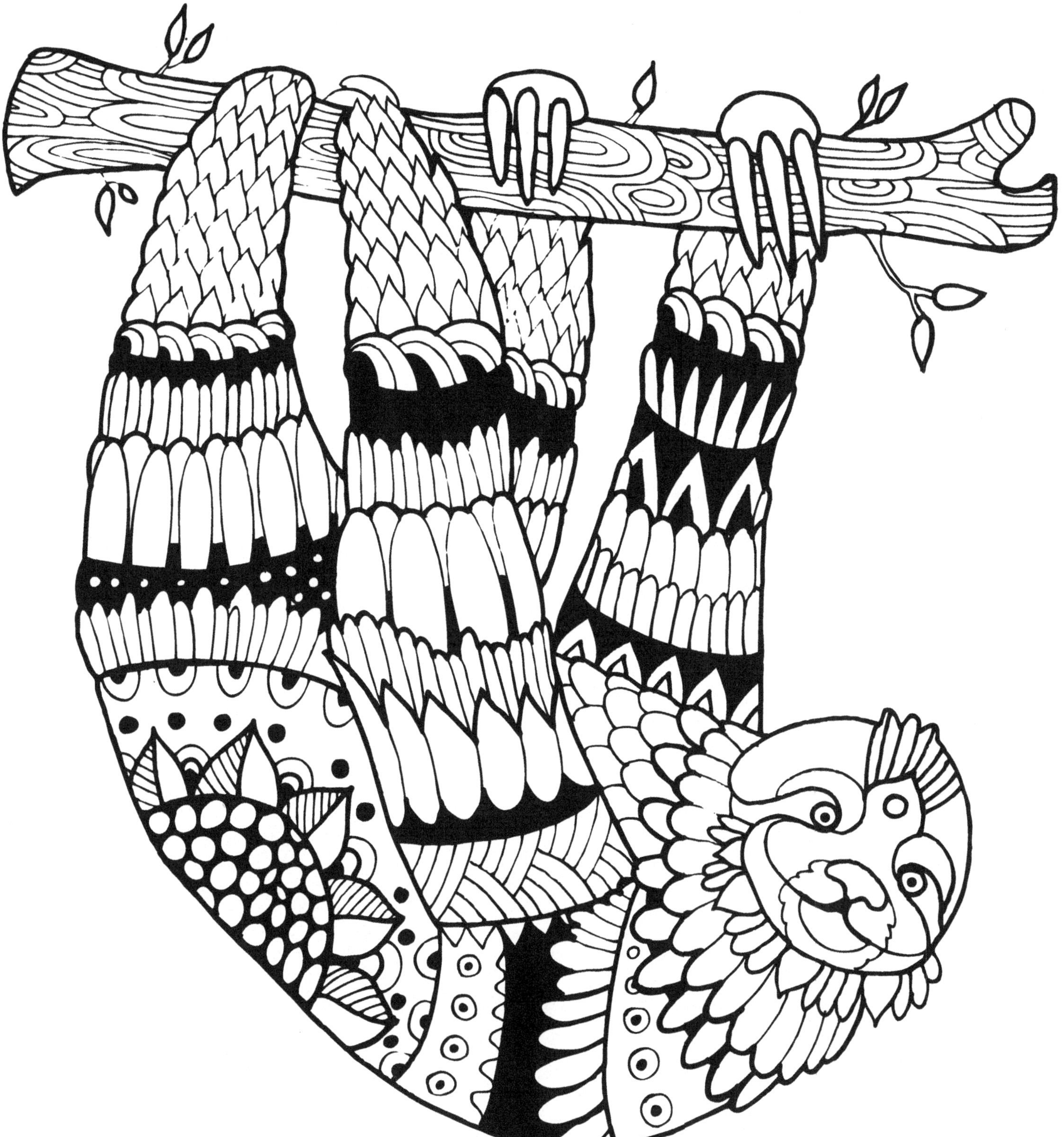

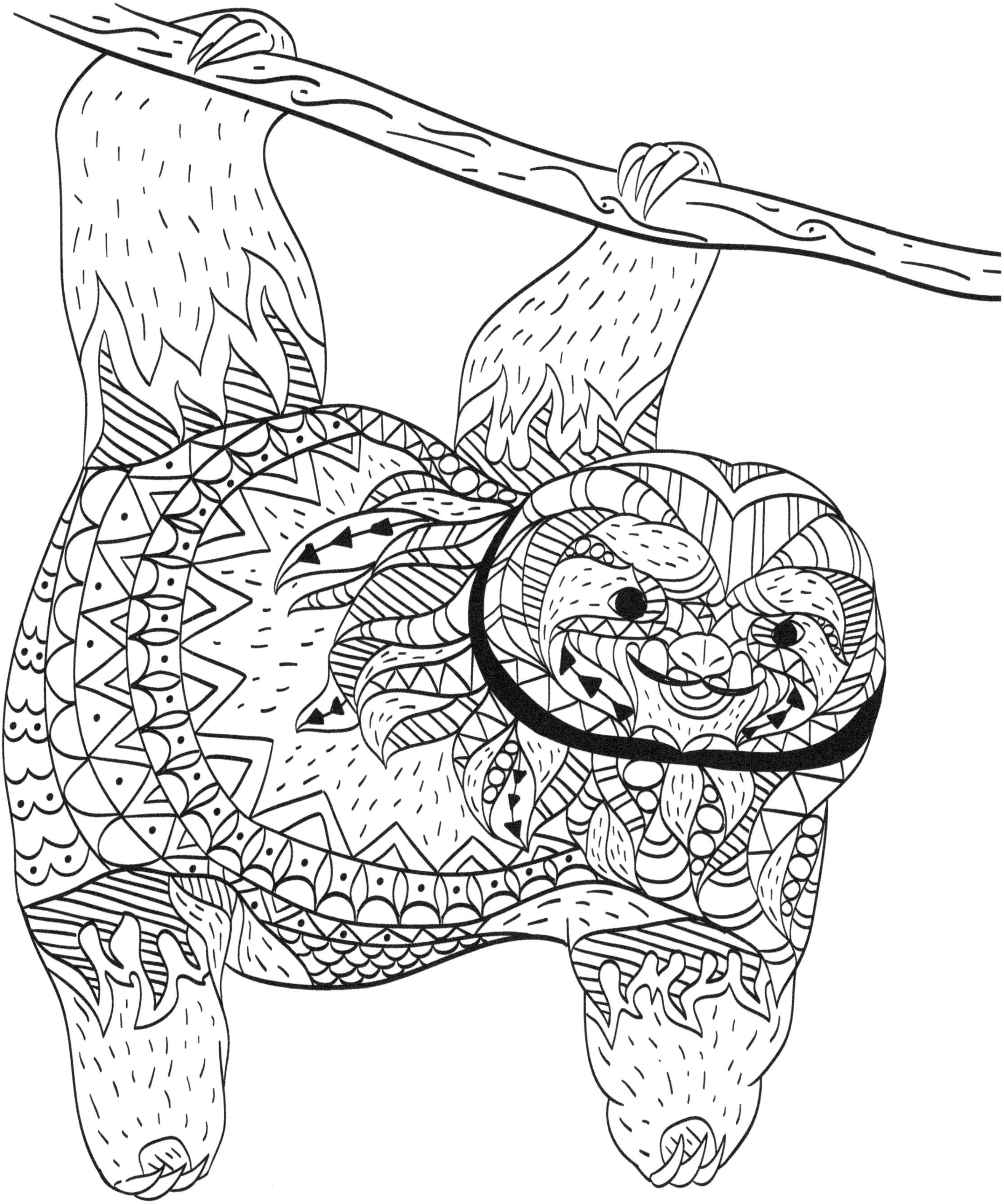

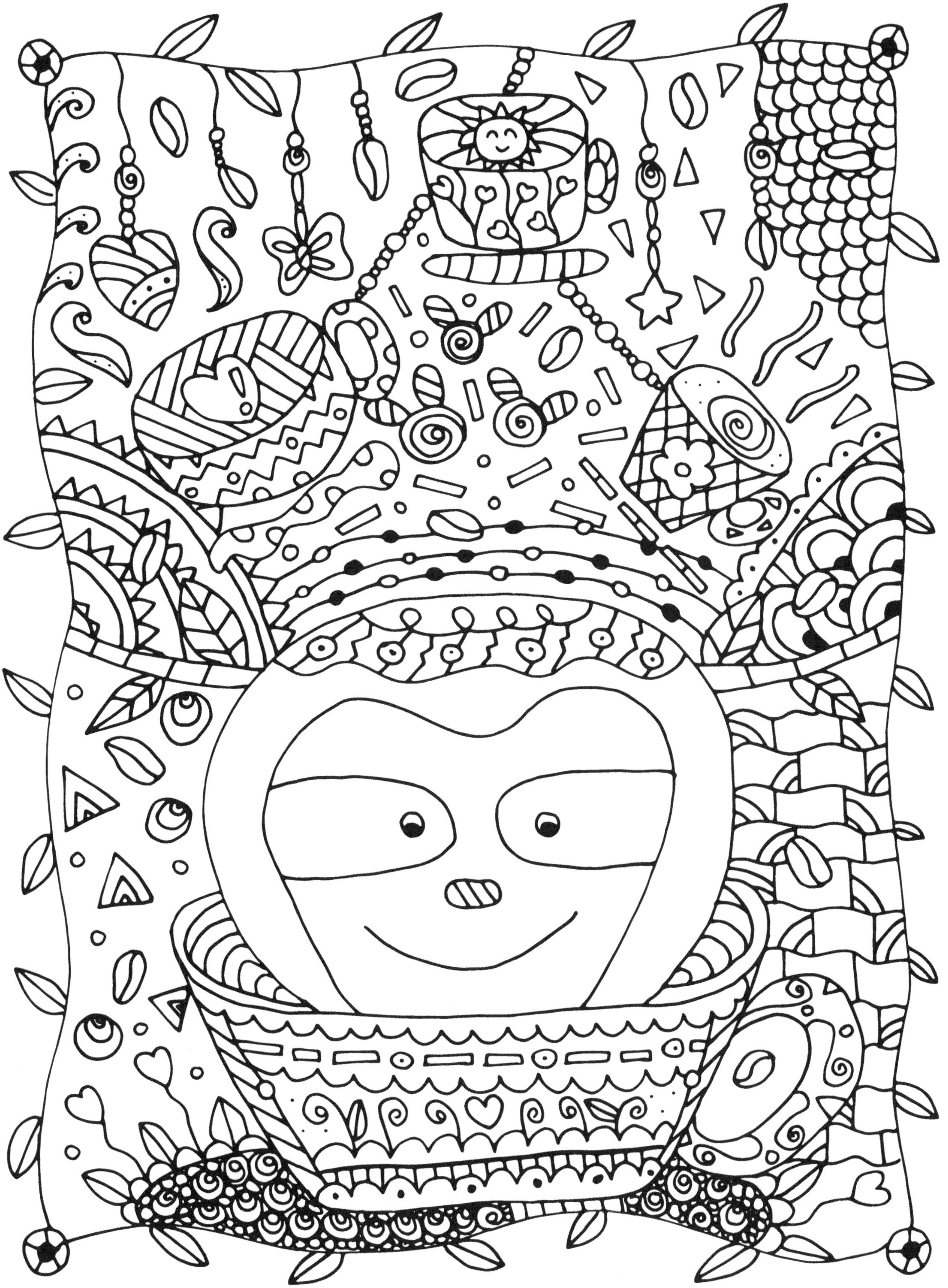

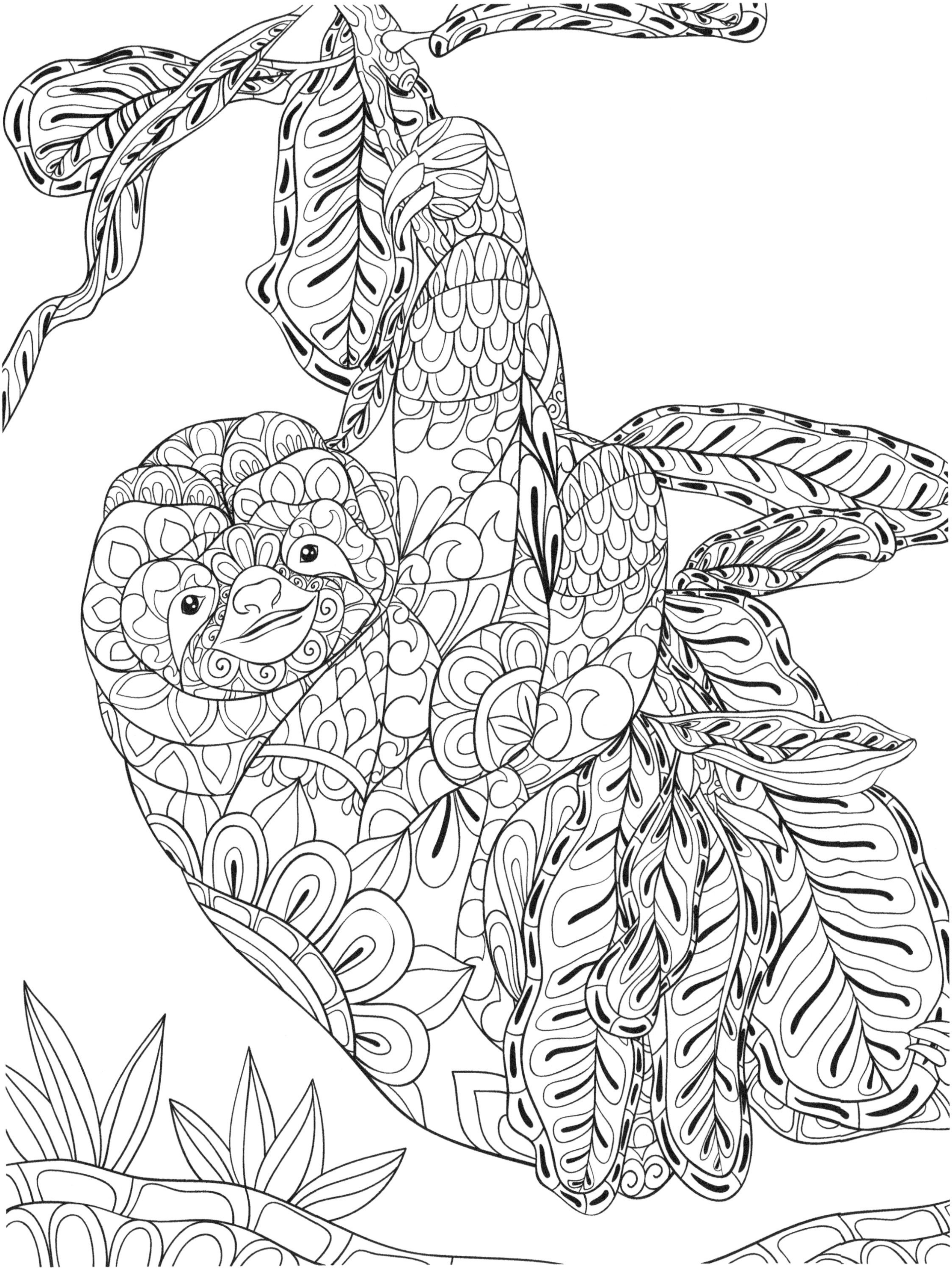

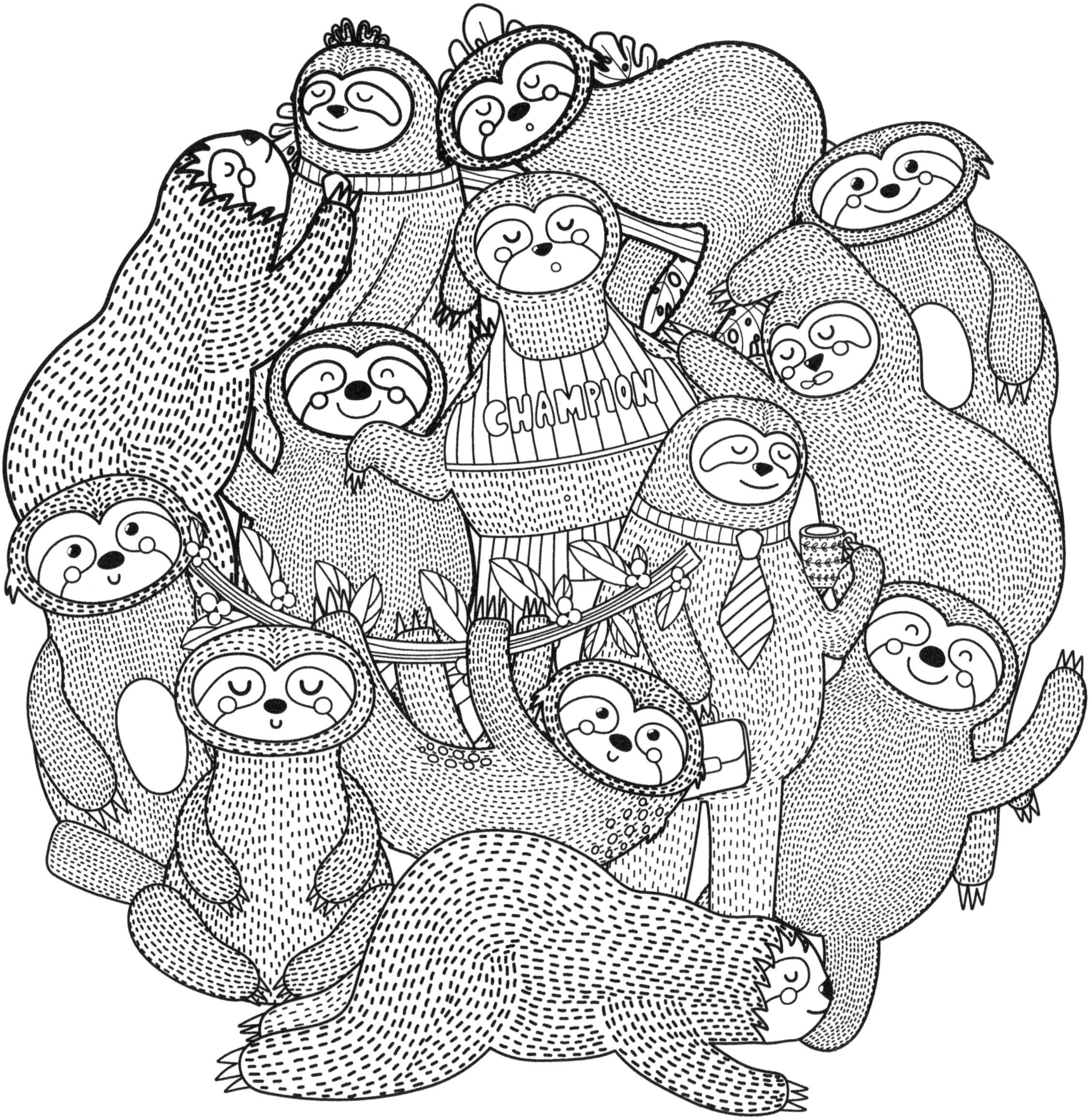
CHAMPION

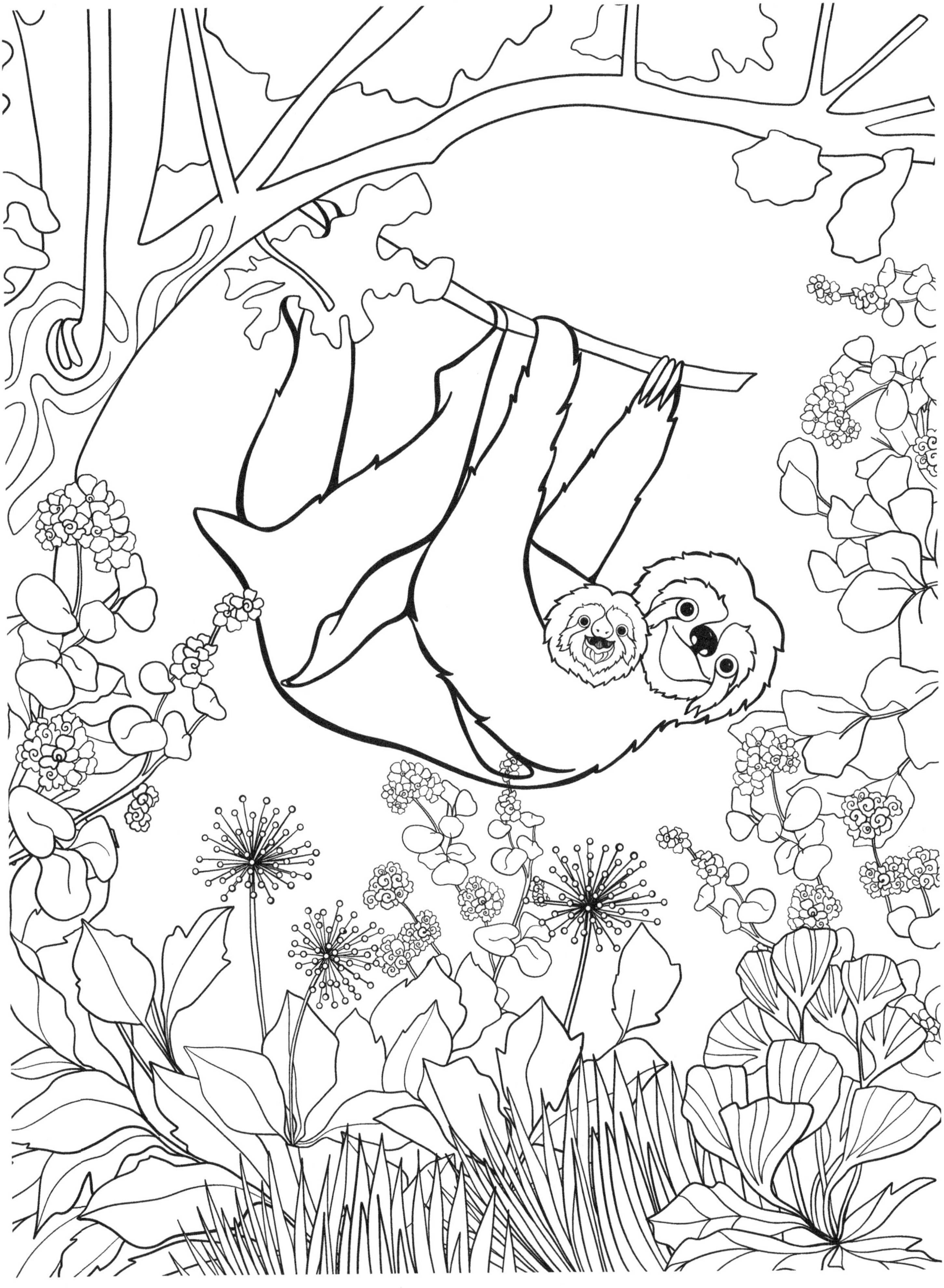

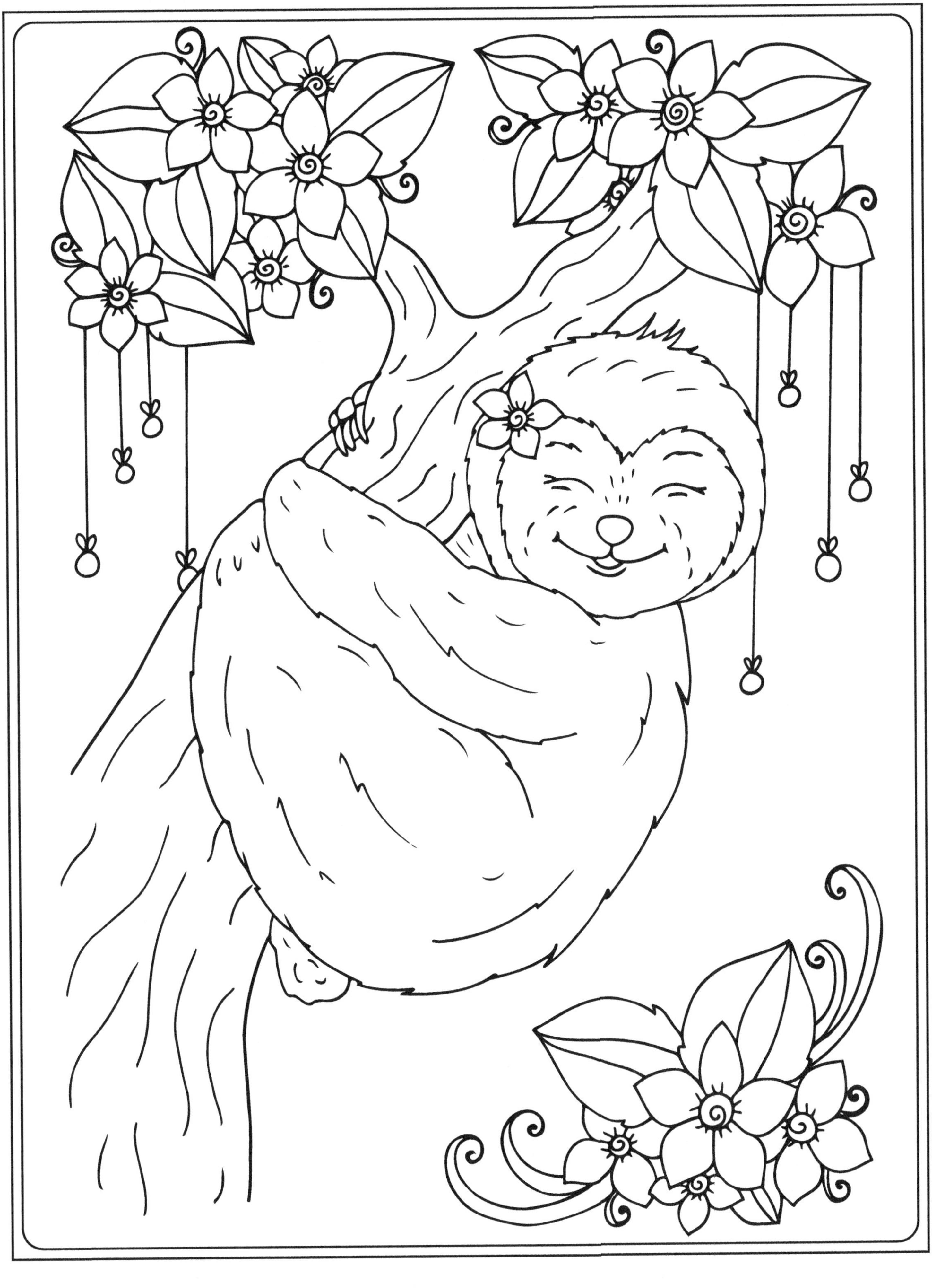

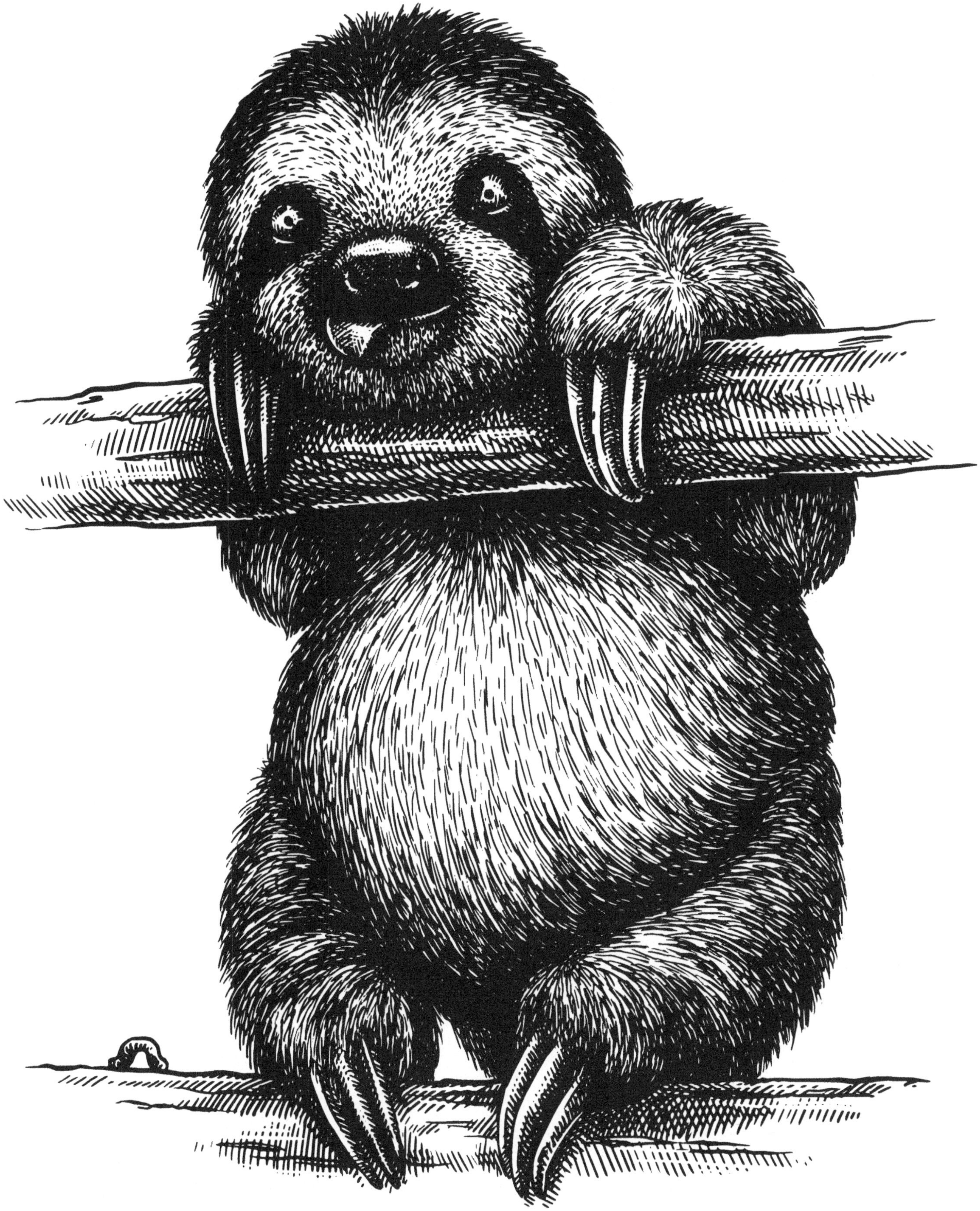

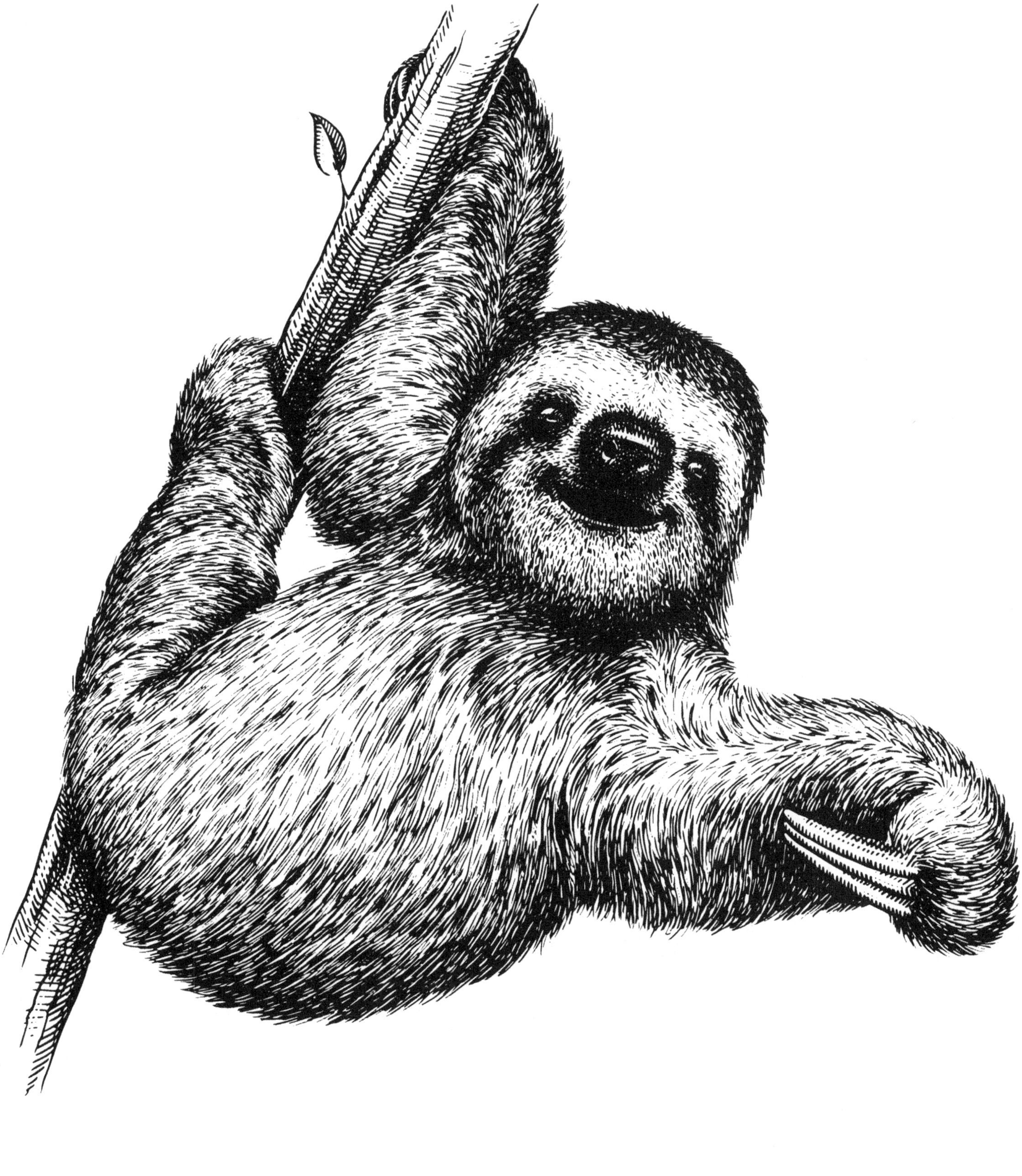

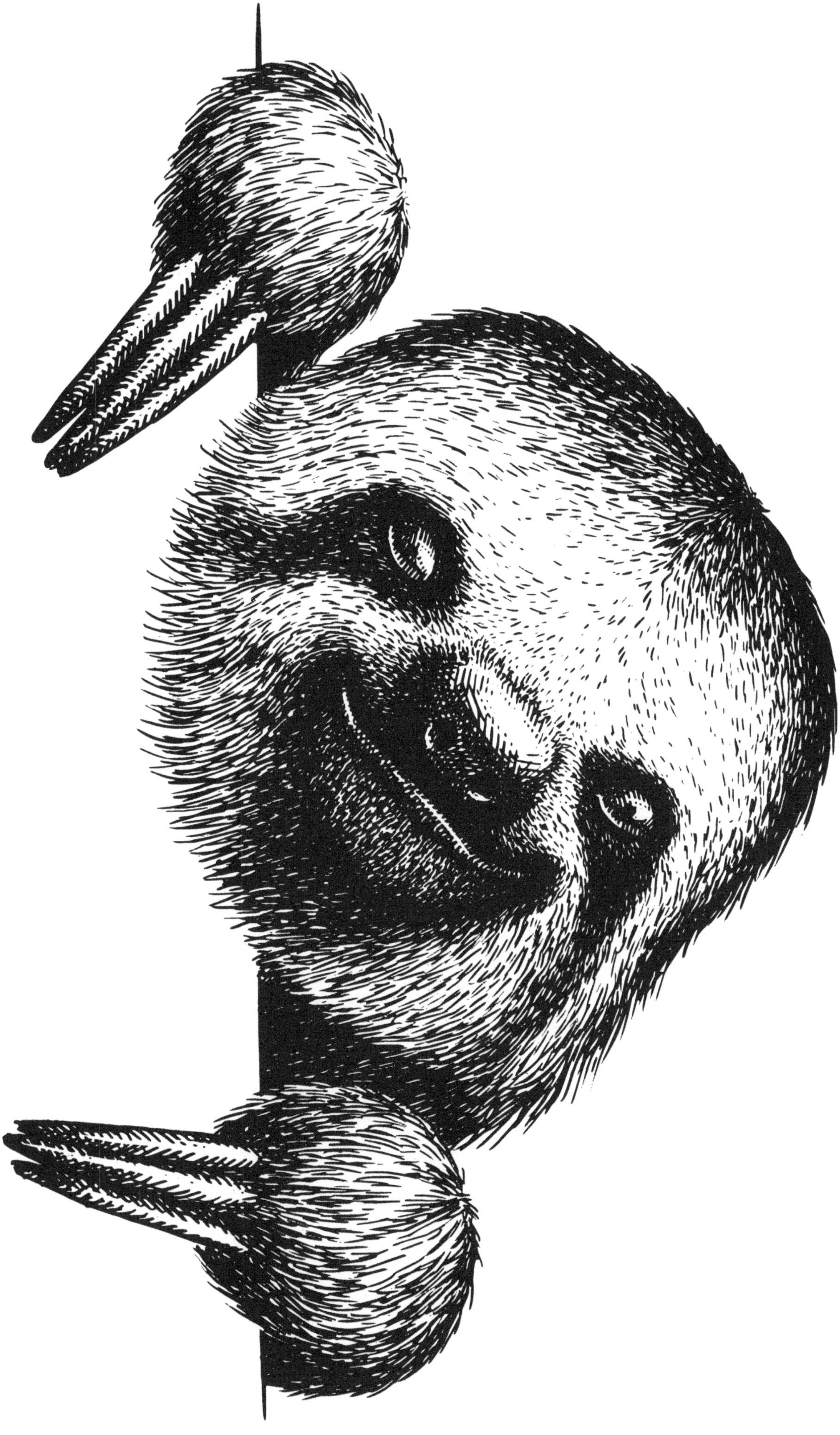

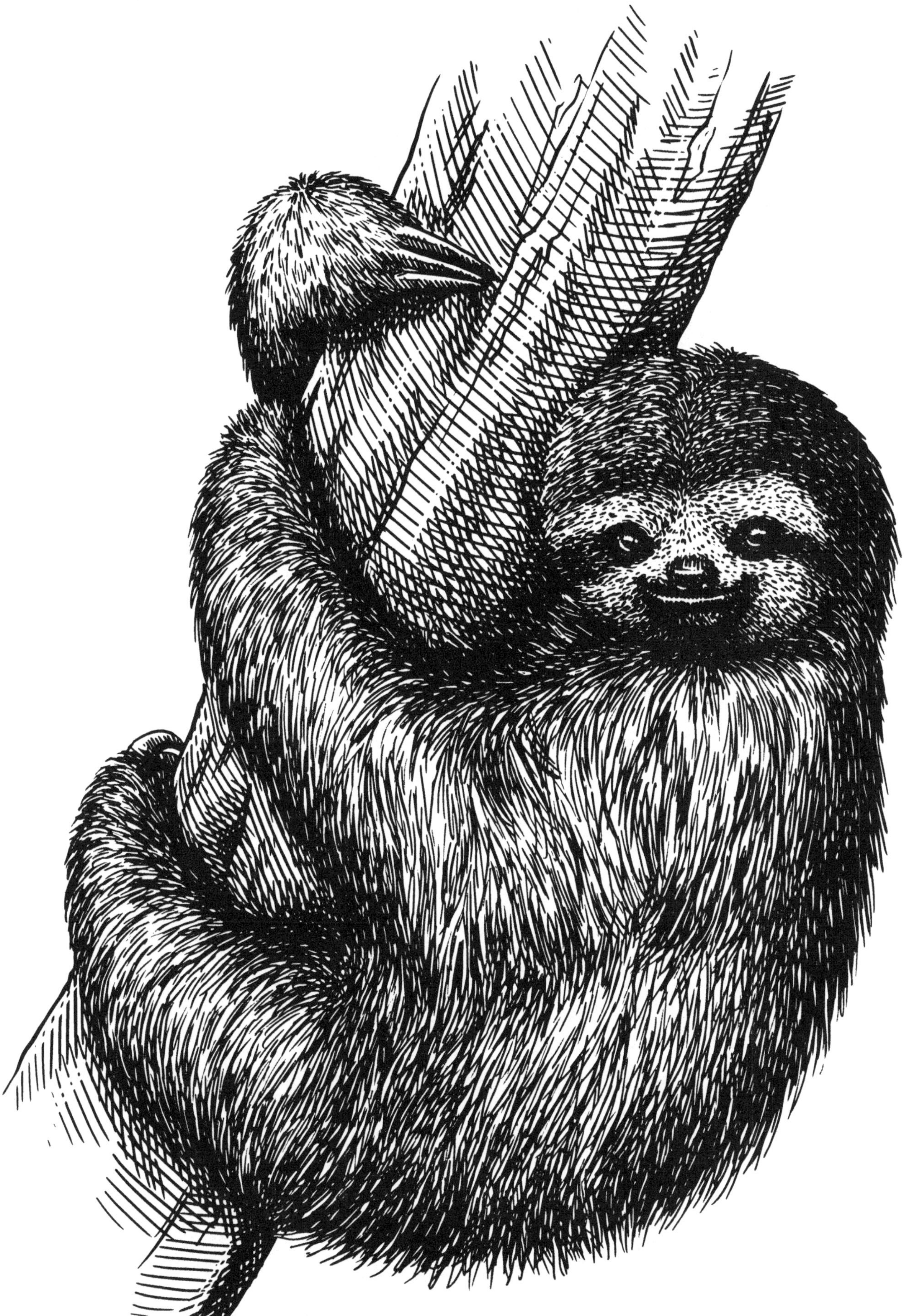

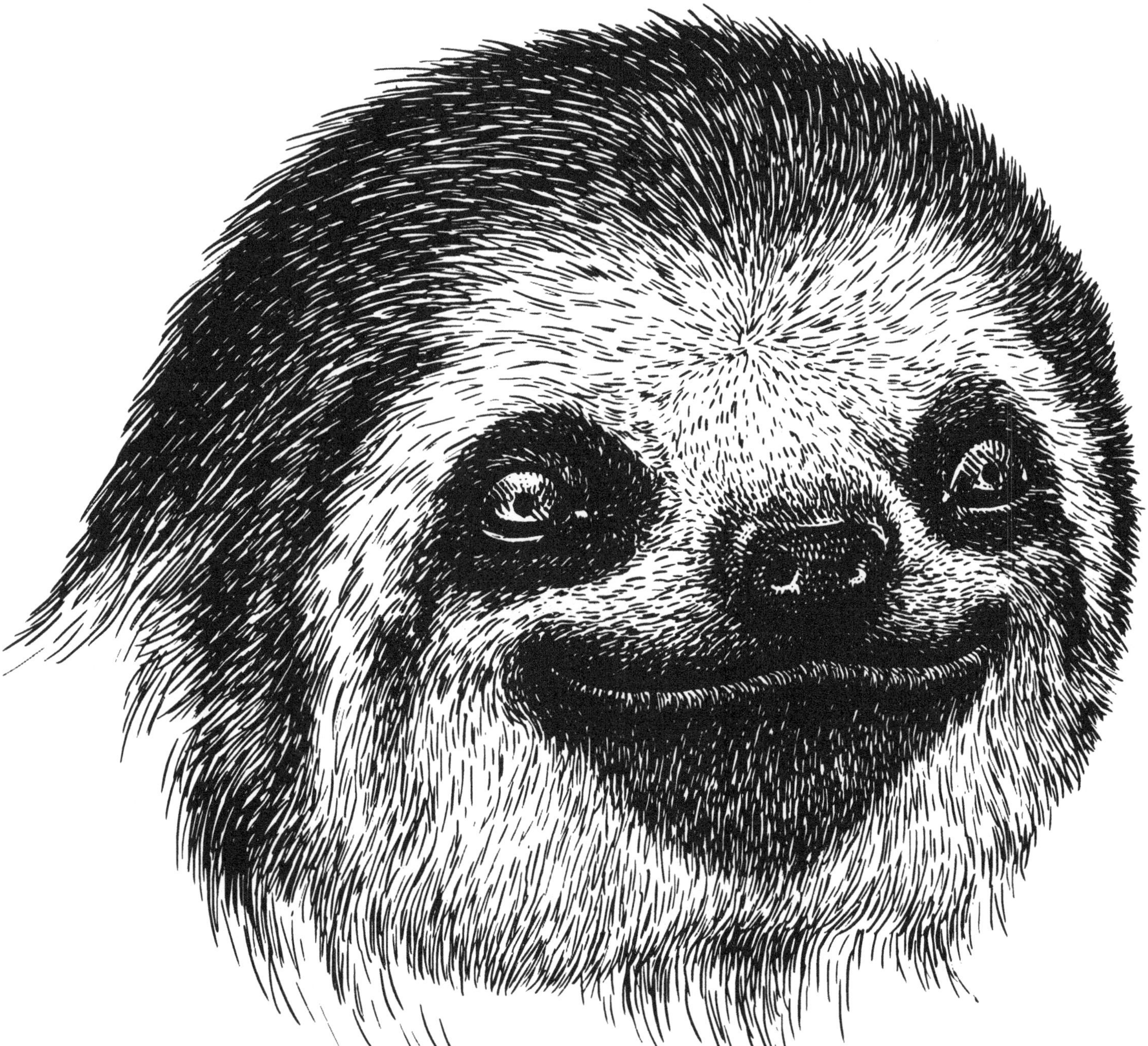

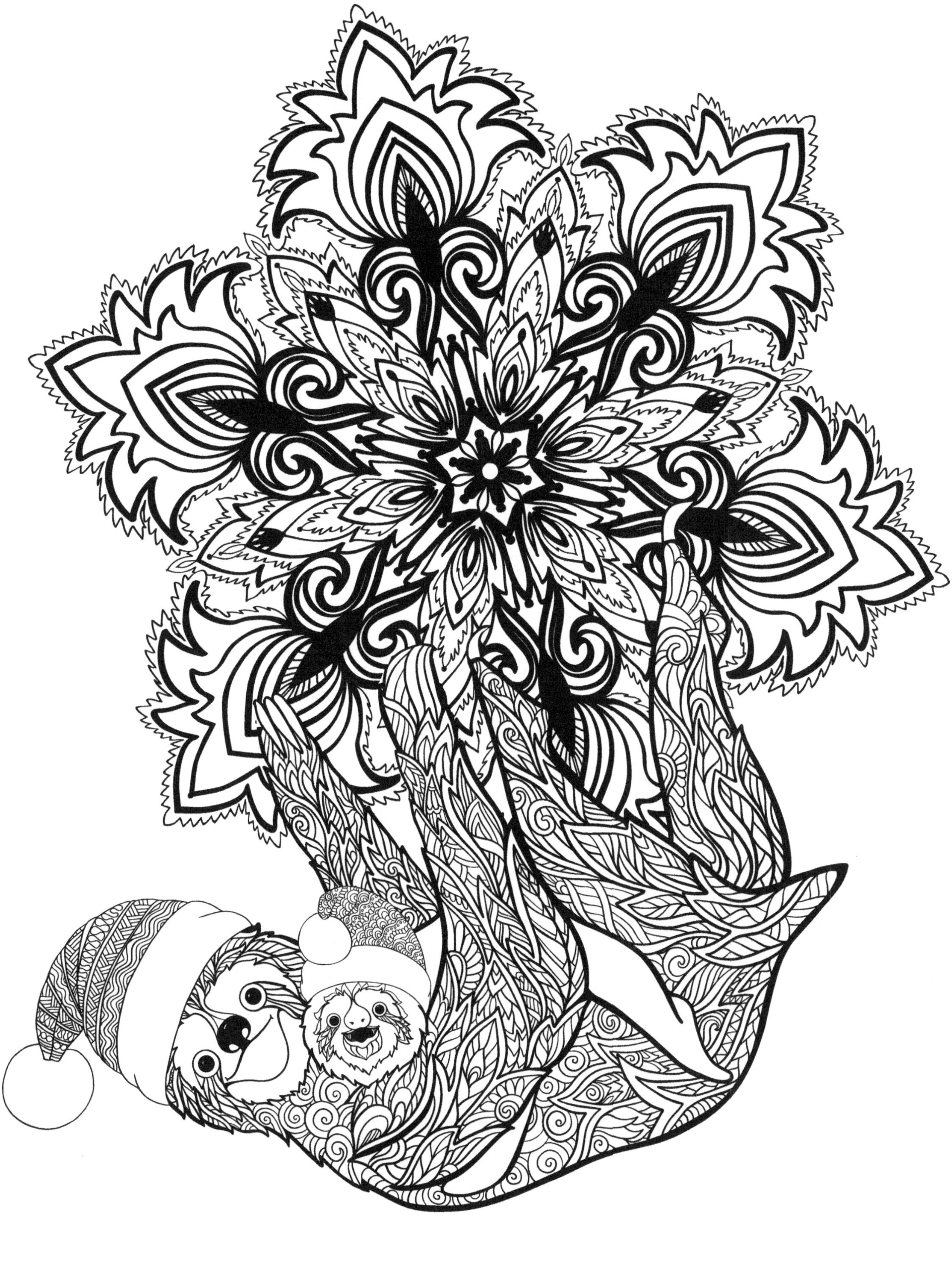

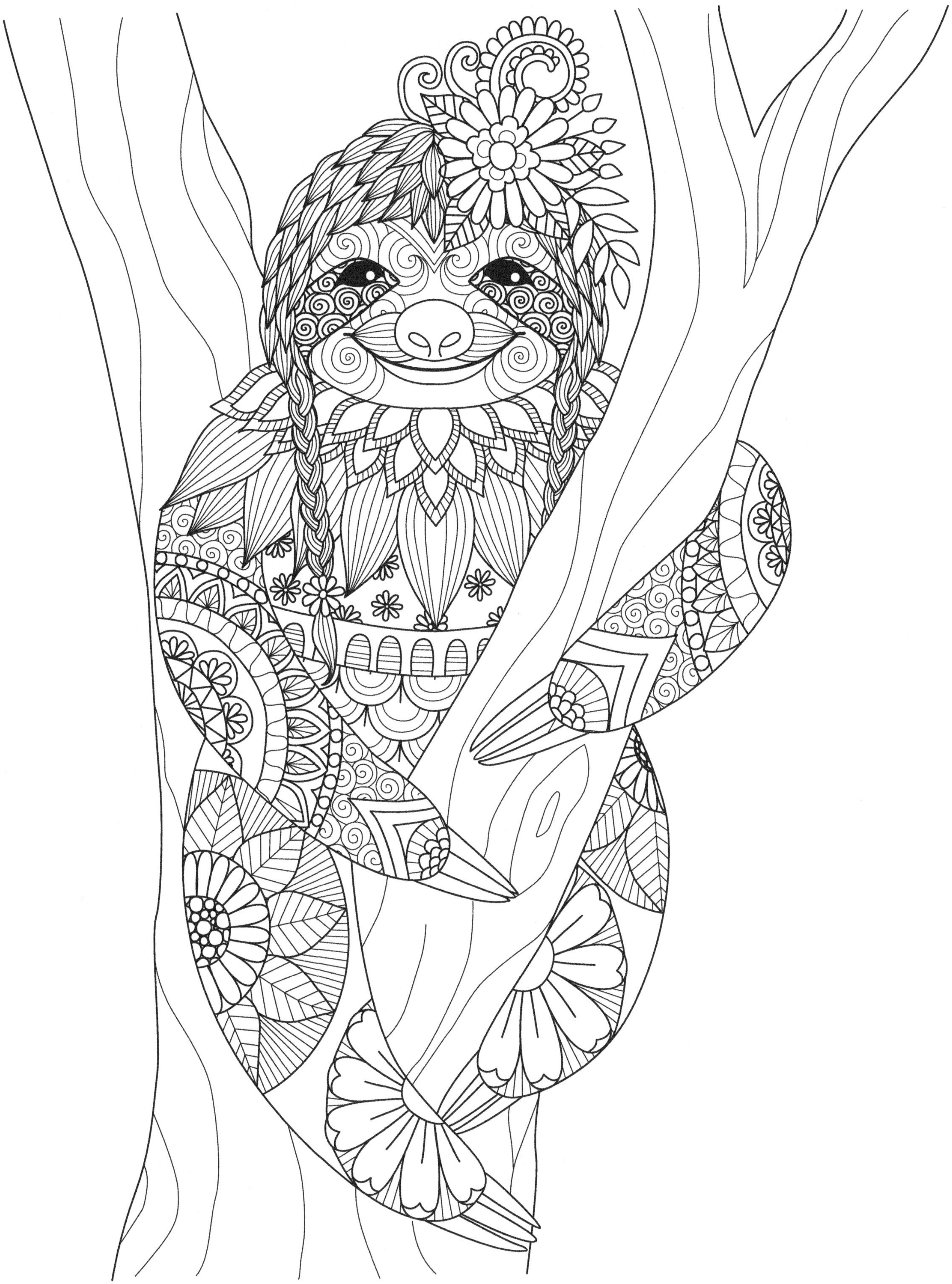

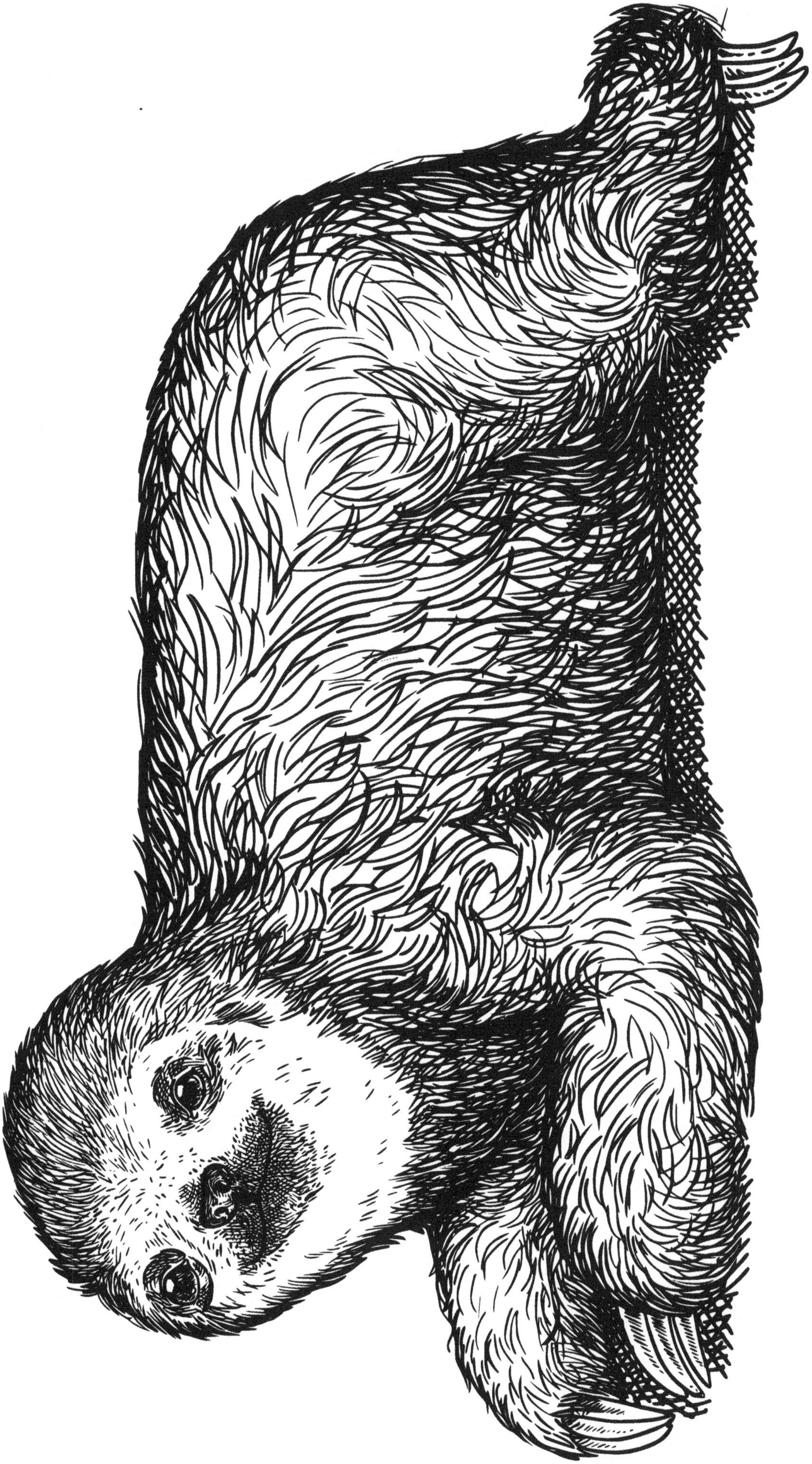

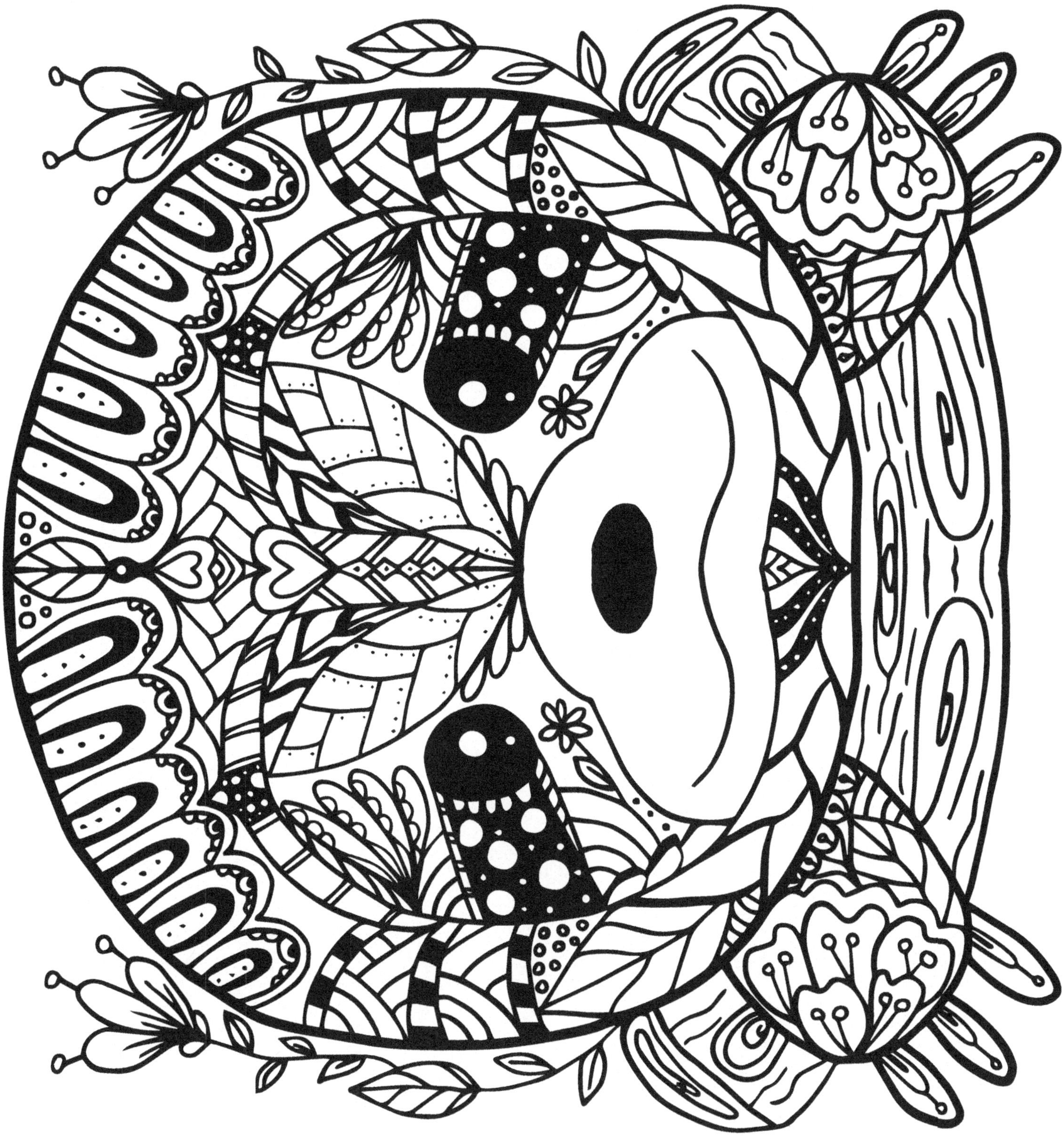

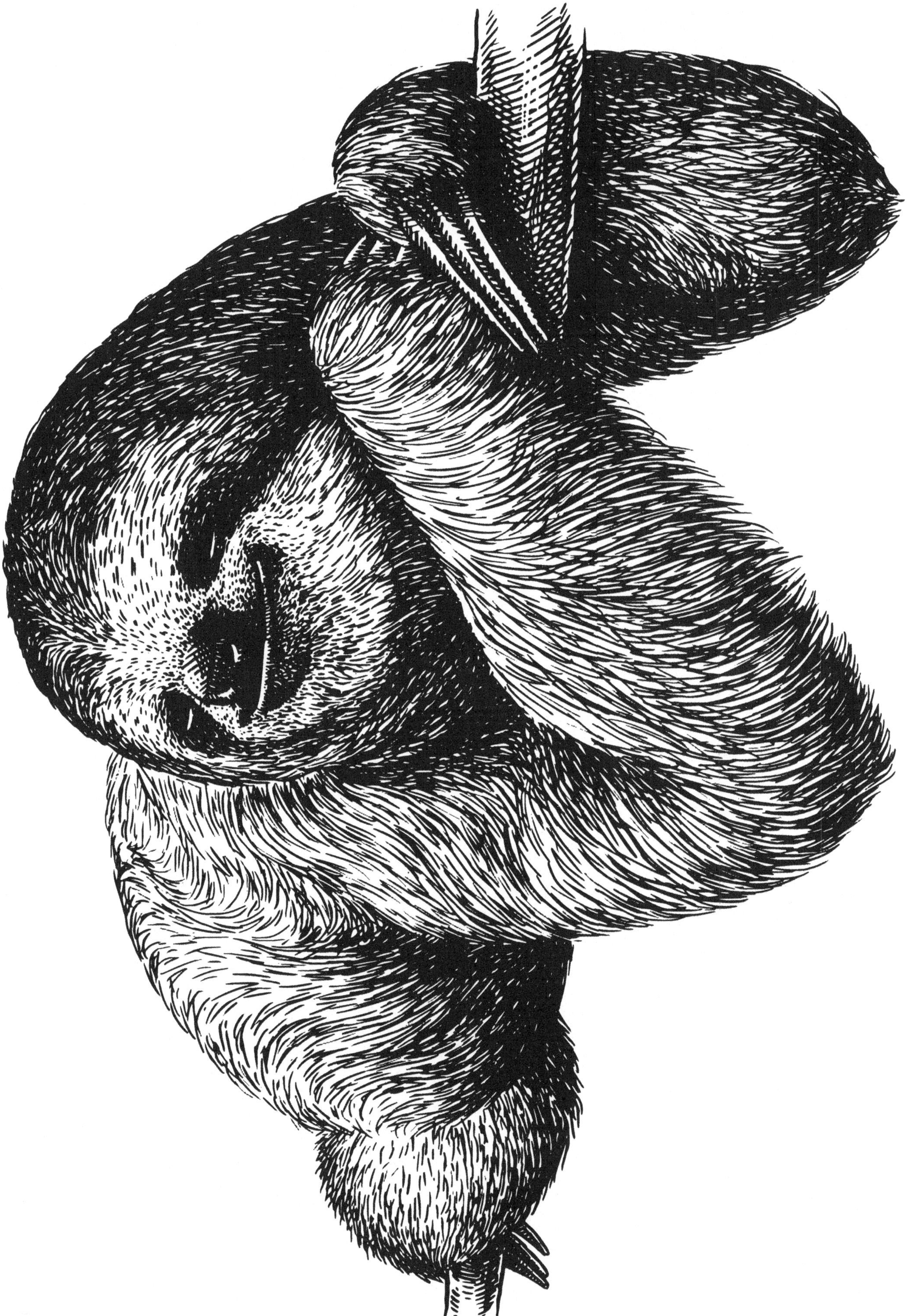

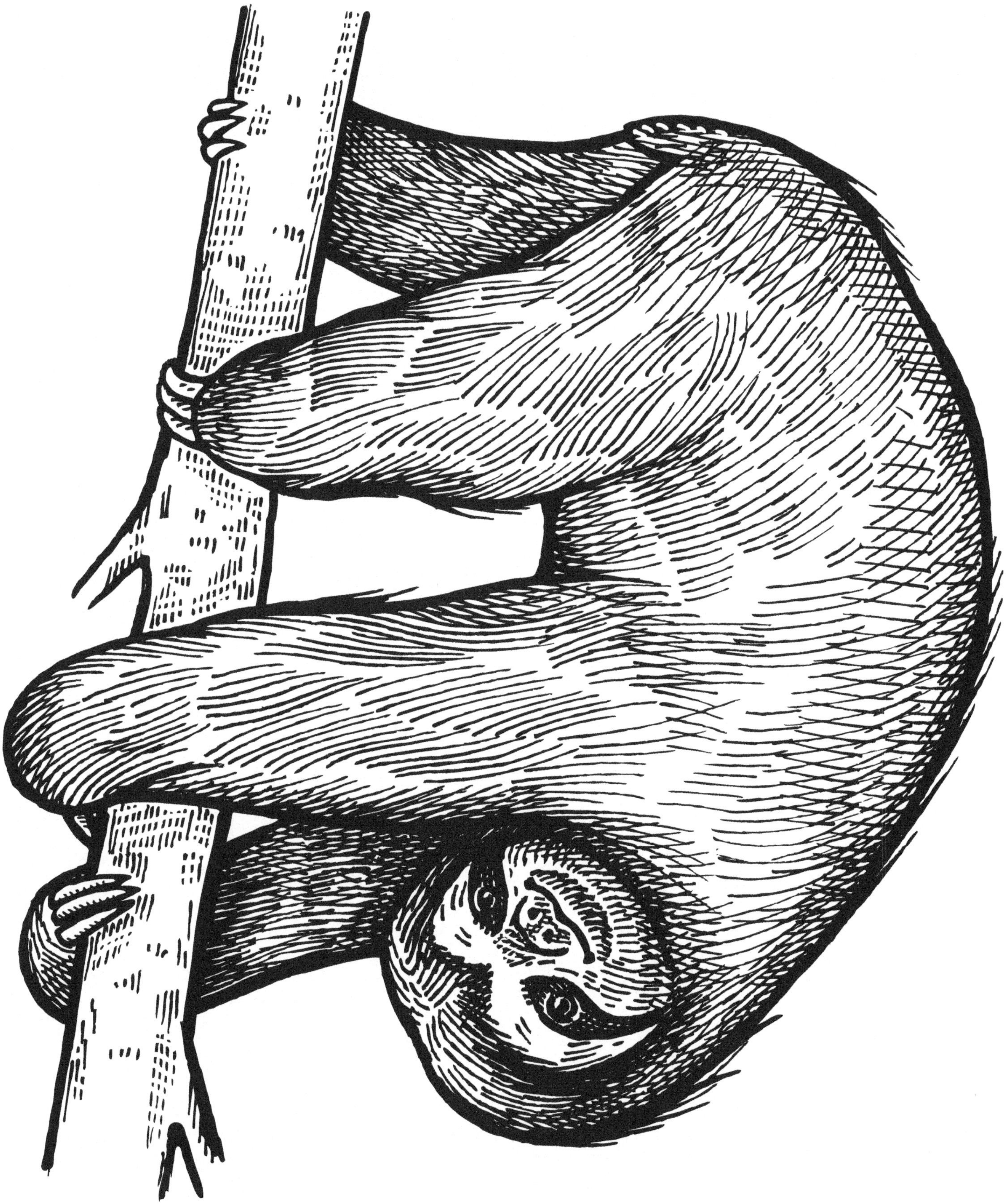

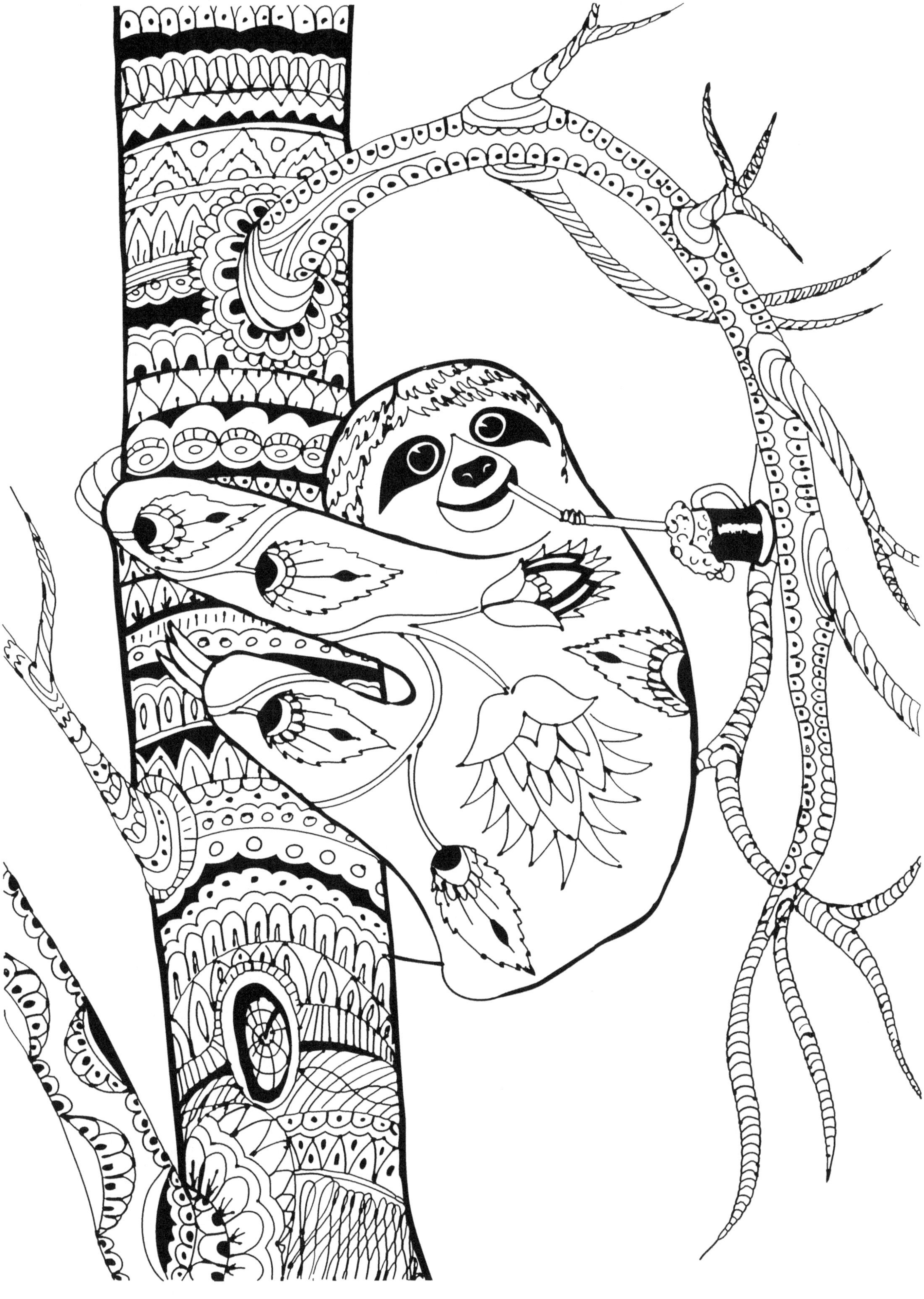

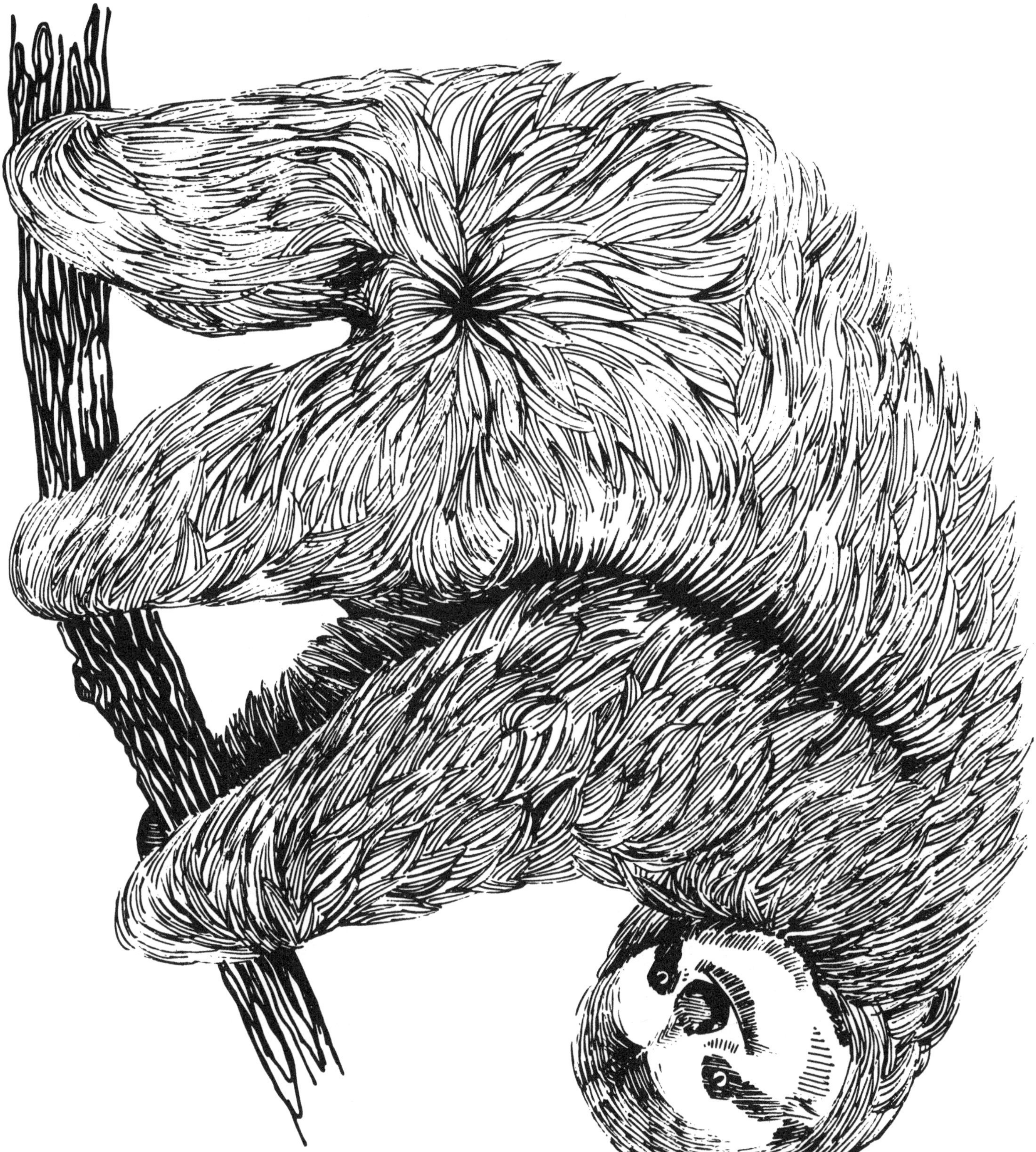

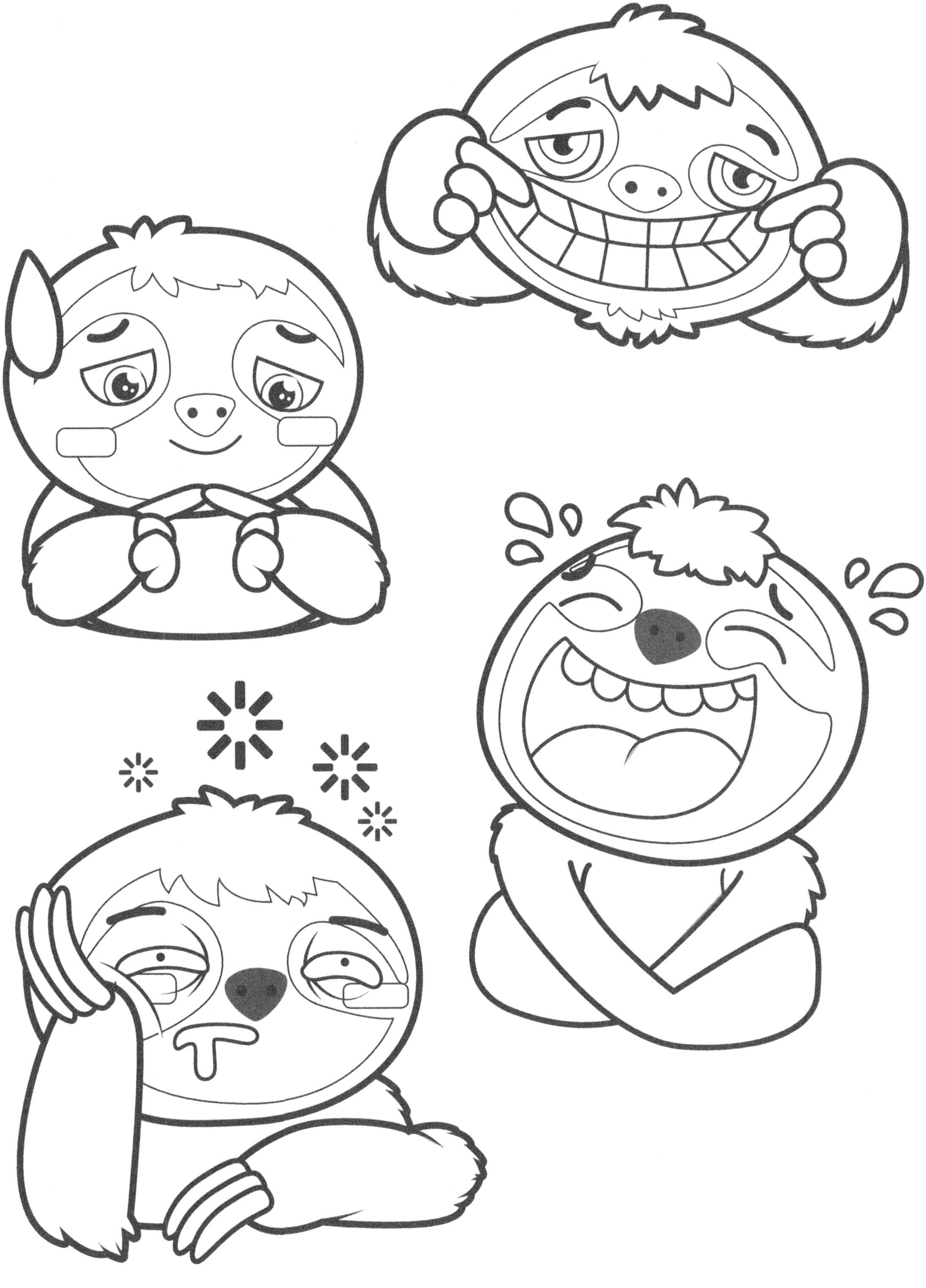

Made in the USA
Middletown, DE
05 November 2021

51674222R00044